EDITOR: Maryanne Blacker

FOOD EDITOR: Pamela Clark

■ ■ ■

ART DIRECTOR: Sue de Guingand

ARTIST: Annemarlene Hissink

■ ■ ■

ASSISTANT FOOD EDITORS: Kathy McGarry,
Louise Patniotis

ASSOCIATE FOOD EDITOR: Enid Morrison

SENIOR HOME ECONOMIST: Lovoni Welch

HOME ECONOMISTS: Janene Brooks, Emma Formica,
Justin Kerr, Maria Sampsonis, Jodie Tilse, Amal Webster

EDITORIAL COORDINATOR: Elizabeth Hooper

KITCHEN ASSISTANT: Amy Wong

■ ■ ■

STYLISTS: Marie-Helene Clauzon, Kay Francis, Jane Hann,
Cherise Koch, Sophia Young

PHOTOGRAPHERS: Robert Clark, Robert Taylor

■ ■ ■

HOME LIBRARY STAFF:

ASSISTANT EDITORS:
Mary-Anne Danaher, Lynne Testoni

EDITORIAL COORDINATOR: Fiona Lambrou

■ ■ ■

CHIEF EXECUTIVE OFFICER: Richard Walsh

PUBLISHER/MANAGING DIRECTOR: Colin Morrison

CIRCULATION & MARKETING DIRECTOR:
Chris Gibson

■ ■ ■

Produced by The Australian Women's Weekly Home Library.
Cover separations by ACP Colour Graphics Pty Ltd., Sydney.
Colour separations by Network Graphics Pty. Ltd., Sydney.
Printing by Hannanprint, Sydney.
Published by ACP Publishing Pty. Limited,
54 Park Street, Sydney.
◆ AUSTRALIA: Distributed by Network Distribution
Company, 54 Park Street Sydney, (02) 282 8777.
◆ UNITED KINGDOM: Distributed in the U.K. by Australian
Consolidated Press (UK) Ltd, 20 Galowhill Rd, Brackmills,
Northampton NN4 7EE (01604) 760 456.
◆ CANADA: Distributed in Canada by Whitecap Books Ltd,
351 Lynn Ave, North Vancouver B.C. V7J 2C4 (604) 980 9852.
◆ NEW ZEALAND: Distributed in New Zealand by Netlink
Distribution Company, 17B Hargreaves St, Level 5,
College Hill, Auckland 1 (9) 302 7616.
◆ SOUTH AFRICA: Distributed in South Africa by Intermag,
PO Box 57394, Springfield 2137, Johannesburg (011) 491 7534.

■ ■ ■

Chinese Cookbook No. 2

Includes index.
ISBN 1 863960 50 3

1. Cookery, Chinese. Title: Australian
Women's Weekly. (Series: Australian
Women's Weekly Home Library).

641.5951

■ ■ ■

© A C P Publishing Pty. Limited 1996
ACN 053 273 546
◆ This publication is copyright. No part of it may be
reproduced or transmitted in any form without the
written permission of the publishers.

■ ■ ■

FRONT COVER: From left: Sesame Lamb Skewers,
page 60; Dim Sim Pouches, page 30;
Prawns and Vegetables with Noodles, page 75.
Ceramic plate from Orson & Blake Collectables;
fans from Made in Japan.
LEFT: Fried Bean Curd and Noodle Soup, page 4.
BACK COVER: Marinated Beef with Spicy
Barbecue Sauce, page 52.

■ ■ ■

CHINESE
COOKBOOK No. 2

Chinese food is always a family favourite and our easy step-by-step recipes show you how to create great-tasting Chinese food at home. In addition to delicious dim sims, stir-fries, meat, vegetable and noodle dishes, there's also an essential guide to rice cooking methods and information about woks. All recipes use ingredients that are readily available from supermarkets or Asian food stores.

D1464027

Pamela Clark

FOOD EDITOR

BRITISH & NORTH AMERICAN READERS: Please note that Australian cup and spoon measurements are metric. A quick conversion guide appears on page 127.
A glossary explaining unfamiliar terms and ingredients appears on page 122.

SOUPS

Chinese food is surely one of the most well-travelled of all cuisines. Its popularity is evidenced by the number of thriving Chinese restaurants in cities and small towns all over the world. China possesses a diversity of cooking styles and tastes and the soups in this chapter represent a number of regions. Stock is an essential ingredient in many Chinese recipes and its flavour is particularly important to soups; our best ever Chinese chicken stock recipe on page 125 will ensure your soups are delicious to the very last drop.

BARBECUED PORK AND VEGETABLE SOUP

2 teaspoons peanut oil
1 clove garlic, crushed
1 small fresh red chilli,
    finely chopped
2 teaspoons grated fresh ginger
1.5 litres (6 cups) chicken stock
5 green shallots, chopped
1 medium (120g) carrot,
    thinly sliced
½ x 425g can straw mushrooms,
    drained, halved
¼ bunch (100g) Chinese
    broccoli, shredded
½ x 425g can baby corn,
    drained, halved
250g Chinese barbecued
    pork, sliced

1. Heat oil in large pan, add garlic, chilli and ginger, cook, stirring, 1 minute. Add stock, shallots and carrot, bring to boil, simmer, uncovered, about 5 minutes or until carrot is tender.

2. Add mushrooms, broccoli, corn and pork, simmer, uncovered, a few minutes or until heated through.
Serves 6.

■ Best made just before serving.
■ Freeze: Not suitable.
■ Microwave: Suitable.

Bowl from House

Fried Bean Curd and Noodle Soup

1 medium (150g) onion, chopped
1 medium (120g) carrot, chopped
1 medium (350g) leek, chopped
2 sticks (200g) celery, chopped
3cm piece fresh ginger,
   peeled, sliced
3 cloves garlic, chopped
2 litres (8 cups) water
1/4 cup (60ml) light soy sauce
2 tablespoons lime juice
pinch Chinese five spice powder
1 medium (120g) carrot, extra
100g snow peas, finely shredded
50g bean thread vermicelli noodles
100g packaged fried bean
   curd, sliced
1/4 cup chopped fresh coriander
   leaves

1. Combine onion, carrot, leek, celery, ginger, garlic and water in large pan, simmer, covered, 1 hour.

2. Strain stock, discard vegetables. Return stock to pan. Add sauce, juice and spice to pan, simmer, uncovered, 5 minutes.

3. Cut extra carrot into thin 5cm sticks. Add carrot, snow peas and noodles to stock, simmer, covered, 2 minutes or until noodles are soft. Just before serving, stir in bean curd and coriander. Serves 4 to 6.

■ Best made just before serving.
■ Freeze: Strained stock suitable.
■ Microwave: Suitable.

CRAB AND SWEET CORN SOUP

2 teaspoons sesame oil
4 green shallots, thinly sliced
1 litre (4 cups) chicken stock
2 x 310g cans creamed corn
1 tablespoon salt-reduced
   soy sauce
1 tablespoon cornflour
1 tablespoon water
250g cooked or canned crab meat

1. Heat oil in large pan, add shallots, cook, stirring, until shallots are soft. Add stock, corn, sauce and blended cornflour and water, stir over heat until mixture boils and thickens slightly.

2. Stir in shredded crab meat, simmer, uncovered, a few minutes or until heated through.
Serves 4.

▓ Best made just before serving.
▓ Freeze: Not suitable.
▓ Microwave: Suitable.

Setting from Storehouse

OMELETTE SURPRISE SOUP

4 Chinese dried mushrooms
60g bean thread vermicelli noodles
2.5 litres (10 cups) chicken stock
2 teaspoons sesame oil
185g minced pork
2 green shallots, finely chopped
1 teaspoon finely grated
   fresh ginger
1½ teaspoons cornflour
2 teaspoons light soy sauce
2 teaspoons oyster sauce
1 tablespoon chopped fresh
   coriander leaves
3 eggs
1 tablespoon water
1 bunch (400g) baby bok
   choy, shredded

3. Whisk eggs and water in bowl until frothy. Heat a lightly oiled 20cm crepe pan, add about 2 tablespoons of egg mixture to pan, swirl to coat base of pan evenly with mixture. Cook until omelette is set on 1 side, carefully slide onto board. Repeat with remaining egg mixture. You need 8 omelettes.

1. Place mushrooms in heatproof bowl, cover with boiling water, stand 20 minutes. Drain mushrooms, discard stems, chop caps finely. Cut noodles into about 4cm lengths with scissors. Reserve ¼ cup (60ml) stock. Bring remaining stock to boil in large pan, add noodles, cook about 2 minutes or until noodles are tender.

4. Place heaped tablespoons of filling on omelettes, fold in sides of omelettes, roll to enclose filling.

2. Heat oil in wok or large pan, add pork, stir-fry until browned. Add mushrooms, shallots and ginger, stir-fry 1 minute. Blend cornflour with reserved stock and sauces, stir into pork mixture, stir over heat until mixture boils and thickens. Stir in coriander; cool.

5. Add omelette parcels and bok choy to stock mixture, simmer, covered, a few minutes or until heated through. Serves 8.

- ■ Recipe best assembled just before serving. Omelettes can be made 3 hours ahead. Pork filling can be made a day ahead.
- ■ Storage: Covered, in refrigerator.
- ■ Freeze: Filling suitable.
- ■ Microwave: Not suitable.

LONG AND SHORT COMBINATION SOUP

6 Chinese dried mushrooms
600g uncooked medium prawns
2 litres (8 cups) chicken stock
1½ cups (115g) finely shredded
   Chinese cabbage
2 tablespoons light soy sauce
2 tablespoons dry sherry
3 green shallots, sliced
½ cup chopped fresh coriander
   leaves
¼ x 375g packet thin fresh
   egg noodles

WONTONS
400g uncooked medium prawns
100g minced pork
2 canned drained water
   chestnuts, chopped
1 clove garlic, chopped
1 teaspoon grated fresh ginger
¼ cup fresh coriander leaves
1 tablespoon salt-reduced
   soy sauce
2 teaspoons dry sherry
18 x 9cm square wonton wrappers
   with egg
1 egg, lightly beaten

1. Place mushrooms in heatproof bowl, cover with boiling water, stand 20 minutes. Drain mushrooms, discard stems, slice caps finely. Shell and devein prawns, leaving tails intact.

2. Heat stock in large pan, add mushrooms, cabbage, sauce, sherry, half the shallots, coriander and wontons. Simmer, uncovered, 5 minutes, add noodles and prawns, simmer, uncovered, few minutes or until prawns are tender. Serve soup sprinkled with remaining shallots.

3. **Wontons:** Shell and devein prawns. Process prawns, pork, water chestnuts, garlic, ginger, coriander, sauce and sherry until mixture forms a paste. Place rounded teaspoons of mixture in centre of wonton wrappers, brush edges lightly with egg.

4. Bring opposite corners into centre of wonton, run fingers along edges of wrapper to seal, forming a parcel. Place wontons on tray, cover, refrigerate until ready to use.
Serves 6.

◼ Wontons can be prepared
  3 hours ahead.
◼ Storage: Covered, in refrigerator.
◼ Freeze: Not suitable.
◼ Microwave: Not suitable.

Basket, mat and spoons from Storehouse; square plates from Made in Japan

ASPARAGUS EGG FLOWER SOUP

500g chicken necks
2.5 litres (10 cups) water
2cm piece fresh ginger,
    peeled, sliced
1 bunch (250g) asparagus
1 tablespoon salt-reduced
    soy sauce
2 green shallots, thinly sliced
2 eggs, lightly beaten
½ teaspoon sesame oil

TOPPING
2 tablespoons dried shrimp,
    chopped
2 teaspoons dried crushed chillies
¼ cup (20g) bottled fried garlic

3. In a slow steady stream, trail combined eggs and oil over surface of gently simmering soup, whisk in quickly to produce thin strands of egg. Serve soup with topping.

1. Discard skin from chicken necks. Combine chicken, water and ginger in large pan. Bring to boil, skim surface, simmer, covered, 2 hours. Strain stock through fine sieve into large bowl, discard necks and ginger, cool. Cover stock, refrigerate overnight.

4. **Topping:** Combine all ingredients in small bowl; mix well.
Serves 4 to 6.

◼ Recipe must be made just before serving. Stock can be made 2 days ahead.
◼ Storage: Covered, in refrigerator.
◼ Freeze: Stock suitable.
◼ Microwave: Not suitable.

2. Next day, skim fat from stock, return stock to pan, bring stock to boil. While stock is heating, snap off and discard tough ends of asparagus; thinly slice asparagus. Add sauce, asparagus and shallots to stock, cook a few minutes or until asparagus is just tender.

TWICE-COOKED FISH SOUP

2 tablespoons cornflour
1 teaspoon Chinese five
   spice powder
1 teaspoon salt
2 x 400g whole bream
vegetable oil for deep-frying
2 litres (8 cups) chicken stock
1/3 cup (70g) canned drained
   bamboo shoots, finely sliced
100g snow peas, finely sliced
1 large (180g) carrot, finely sliced
1 small (200g) leek, finely sliced
2½ tablespoons salt-reduced
   soy sauce
2½ tablespoons rice vinegar
¼ cup chopped fresh
   coriander leaves

1. Place combined cornflour, spice and salt in plastic bag, add whole fish separately to bag, shake well to coat fish with mixture. Heat oil in wok or large pan, deep-fry fish separately 1 minute each side; drain on absorbent paper.

2. Add stock to large pan, bring to boil, add vegetables, sauce, vinegar and coriander. Reduce heat, add fish carefully, simmer, uncovered, about 5 minutes or until vegetables are just tender. Lift fish into large serving dish, pour soup over fish.
Serves 6.

■ Best made just before serving.
■ Freeze: Not suitable.
■ Microwave: Not suitable.

Setting from Storehouse

Prawn Dumpling Soup with Chilli Paste

350g uncooked medium prawns
200g minced pork
2 green shallots, finely chopped
35 x 9cm square wonton wrappers
   with egg
2 litres (8 cups) chicken stock
1 tablespoon rice wine
2 teaspoons salt-reduced soy sauce
¼ teaspoon sesame oil
½ bunch (175g) tat-soi leaves

CHILLI PASTE
6 small fresh red chillies, chopped
2 cloves garlic
1 tablespoon chopped fresh
   coriander stems
1 teaspoon peanut oil
1 teaspoon white vinegar

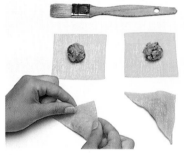

1. Shell and devein prawns; chop finely. Combine prawns, pork and shallots in bowl; mix well. Place rounded teaspoons of mixture in centres of wonton wrappers, brush edges with a little water. Fold wrappers in half diagonally to form triangular dumplings, pinch edges together to seal.

Setting from Storehouse

2. Drop dumplings into large pan of boiling water, simmer, uncovered, about 5 minutes or until tender. Lift dumplings onto tray using a slotted spoon, cover, refrigerate until required.

3. Combine stock, wine, sauce and oil in large pan, cover, bring to boil. Drop cooked dumplings into stock mixture, add tat-soi leaves, simmer, uncovered, until heated through. Serve soup with chilli paste.

4. **Chilli Paste:** Using a mortar and pestle, grind all ingredients together until smooth.
Serves 4 to 6.

■ Recipe best assembled just before serving. Prawn dumplings can be made 3 hours ahead. Chilli paste can be made a day ahead.
■ Storage: Covered, in refrigerator.
■ Freeze: Not suitable.
■ Microwave: Not suitable.

ENTREES

Chinese cooking emphasises the harmonious blending of flavours, versatile ingredients and contrasting textures and colours. Mix and match our recipes; you'll find that these entrees would be equally appetising as stand-alone snacks or as part of a grand banquet. Remember, too, preparation is all important, it's usually the time-consuming part, the cooking time is quick.

SALT AND PEPPER BUTTERFLIED PRAWNS

4 x 9cm square wonton wrappers
1kg uncooked medium prawns
vegetable oil for shallow-frying
1 tablespoon peanut oil
2 cloves garlic, crushed
1 small fresh red chilli, sliced
1 tablespoon lime juice
2 tablespoons mild sweet
  chilli sauce
3 green shallots, thinly sliced
2 teaspoons sesame seeds, toasted

SEASONING
½ teaspoon black peppercorns
¼ teaspoon coriander seeds
¾ teaspoon sea salt flakes
¼ teaspoon lemon pepper
  seasoning

1. Cut wonton wrappers in half diagonally. Shell prawns, leaving tails intact. Cut prawns down the back, cutting nearly all the way through; remove veins, flatten prawns slightly.

2. Shallow-fry wonton wrappers in hot vegetable oil in batches until lightly browned; drain on absorbent paper. Shallow-fry prawns in hot oil in batches about 30 seconds or until prawns are almost tender and have changed colour; drain on absorbent paper.

3. Heat peanut oil in wok or pan, add garlic and chilli, stir-fry until fragrant. Add prawns, juice, sauce and seasoning mixture, stir-fry until heated through. Stir in shallots, sprinkle with seeds. Serve with wontons.

4. Seasoning: Lightly crush peppercorns and seeds, add salt and lemon pepper.

Serves 4 to 6.
- Best made just before serving.
- Freeze: Not suitable.
- Microwave: Not suitable.

PORK BALLS WITH CHILLI SAUCE

4 Chinese dried mushrooms
600g minced pork
1 medium (150g) onion,
    finely chopped
2 cloves garlic, crushed
1 tablespoon grated fresh ginger
4 canned drained water chestnuts,
    finely chopped
3/4 cup (50g) stale breadcrumbs
1/2 cup (75g) cornflour
2 tablespoons salt-reduced
    soy sauce
1 egg, lightly beaten
1/3 cup chopped fresh
    coriander leaves
vegetable oil for deep-frying

CHILLI SAUCE
2 teaspoons peanut oil
1 clove garlic, crushed
4 green shallots, chopped
1 teaspoon chilli oil
2 tablespoons salt-reduced
    soy sauce
1 tablespoon hoisin sauce
1 tablespoon black bean sauce
2 tablespoons rice vinegar
1/2 cup (125ml) chicken stock
1 teaspoon cornflour
2 teaspoons water

1. Place mushrooms in small heat-proof bowl, cover with boiling water, stand 20 minutes. Drain mushrooms, discard stems, chop caps finely.

2. Combine pork, mushrooms, onion, garlic, ginger, chestnuts, breadcrumbs, half the cornflour, sauce, egg and coriander in large bowl; mix well. Cover, refrigerate 1 hour.

3. Roll tablespoons of pork mixture into balls, lightly coat with remaining cornflour. Deep-fry pork balls in hot oil in batches until cooked through; drain on absorbent paper. Serve warm with chilli sauce.

4. Chilli Sauce: Heat peanut oil in pan, add garlic and shallots, cook, stirring, 1 minute. Stir in chilli oil, sauces, vinegar and stock, then blended cornflour and water, stir over heat until sauce boils and thickens.
Makes about 45.

■ Recipe can be prepared
  a day ahead.
■ Storage: Covered, separately,
  in refrigerator.
■ Freeze: Cooked pork balls suitable.
■ Microwave: Not suitable.

CRISPY CHICKEN WITH HONEY SAUCE

400g chicken thigh fillets
1/3 cup (50g) plain flour
1/3 cup (80ml) water
1 1/2 tablespoons peanut oil
2 egg whites
vegetable oil for deep-frying
2 green shallots

HONEY SAUCE
1 tablespoon peanut oil
2 cloves garlic, crushed
1 tablespoon grated fresh ginger
2 tablespoons salt-reduced
    soy sauce
1/4 cup (60ml) honey
1 tablespoon dry sherry
1/3 cup (80ml) chicken stock
1 1/2 teaspoons cornflour
1 teaspoon water

1. Cut chicken into 2cm pieces. Whisk flour with water in medium bowl, whisk in peanut oil, whisk until smooth; stand 30 minutes.

2. Beat egg whites in small bowl until soft peaks form, gently fold into flour mixture in 2 batches. Dip chicken pieces into batter, deep-fry in hot vegetable oil in batches about 5 minutes or until browned and tender (do not have oil too hot or coating will overbrown before chicken is cooked). Drain on absorbent paper.

3. Cut green part of shallots into 2cm lengths. Make fine cuts close together at 1 end of each length to make frills. Place hot chicken pieces and shallot frills on toothpicks, serve with honey sauce.

4. **Honey Sauce:** Heat oil in small pan, add garlic and ginger, cook, stirring, 1 minute. Add sauce, honey, sherry and stock, cook, stirring, about 3 minutes or until slightly thickened. Stir in blended cornflour and water, stir over heat until mixture boils and thickens.
Makes about 40.

■ Best made just before serving.
■ Freeze: Not suitable.
■ Microwave: Not suitable.

Plum 'n' Garlic-Glazed Pork Spare Ribs

1kg American-style pork spare ribs
2 tablespoons salt-reduced
soy sauce
1 tablespoon hoisin sauce
½ cup (125ml) plum sauce
1 tablespoon honey
2 teaspoons sesame oil
2 cloves garlic, crushed
2 teaspoons grated fresh ginger
2 tablespoons rice vinegar

1. Cut ribs into serving-sized pieces. Combine remaining ingredients in large bowl, add ribs; mix well. Cover, refrigerate 3 hours or overnight.

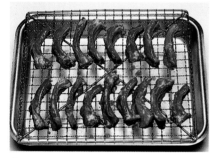

2. Place ribs on wire rack over baking dish. Pour enough boiling water into dish to just cover base. Bake, uncovered, in moderate oven about 45 minutes or until ribs are tender.
Serves 4.

■ Best cooked just before serving.
■ Freeze: Marinated ribs suitable.
■ Microwave: Not suitable.

Chinese lantern and plate from Eastern Flair; fabric from St James Furnishings

STEAMED DUMPLINGS

■ *Soft, light pastry encases tasty fillings in these treats. We have made 5 fillings and 2 dipping sauces, and we show you how to shape the dumplings in different ways.*

■ *Fillings and dipping sauces can be made a day ahead, cover and refrigerate them.*

■ *The pastry is best made close to assembling, and dumplings must be cooked just before serving. Each filling makes enough for 24 dumplings. Dumplings are not suitable to freeze; fillings are suitable to microwave.*

BASIC PASTRY

1 cup (150g) plain flour
¼ cup (35g) cornflour
1 cup (250ml) water
1 tablespoon vegetable oil
2 tablespoons sesame oil

1. Sift flours into medium bowl. Combine water and vegetable oil in small pan, bring to boil, pour over flours, stirring quickly with a wooden spoon to mix to a sticky dough.

2. Knead dough briefly on lightly floured baking paper until smooth. Divide dough into 5 portions; wrap each portion in plastic. Roll each portion between sheets of baking paper until about 1mm thick (pastry should be paper thin, almost see-through). Cut 4 x 9 cm rounds from each portion of dough. Re-roll all scraps, cut 4 more 9cm rounds. Drop rounded teaspoons of filling into centres of rounds.

3. Crescents: Fold rounds over to enclose filling and make crescents; press edges together to seal. Using fingers, crimp edges.

4. Pouches: Gather dough around filling and twist to seal. For a variation, turn dumpling upside down so the twist becomes the base.

5. Pockets: Using both hands, pinch rounds together as shown; press edges together.

6. Line a large bamboo steamer with baking paper. Place dumplings in batches in steamer, brush lightly with sesame oil, cover, steam over wok or pan of simmering water about 10 minutes or until pastry is translucent. Serve with dipping sauces.

FILLINGS

DUCK AND BLACK BEAN
250g Chinese barbecued duck
2 teaspoons peanut oil
1 clove garlic, crushed
3 green shallots, finely chopped
80g mushrooms, finely chopped
2 tablespoons black bean sauce
2 tablespoons water
1 teaspoon sugar

Discard skin and bones from duck, chop meat finely (you need 1 cup meat). Heat oil in small pan, add garlic, shallots and mushrooms, cook, stirring, until mushrooms are soft. Stir in remaining ingredients, cook, stirring, 2 minutes; cool.

PRAWN AND BOK CHOY
2 teaspoons peanut oil
2 green shallots, finely chopped
1 teaspoon grated fresh ginger
1/2 small (35g) carrot, finely grated
2 teaspoons chopped fresh
**   coriander leaves**
2 tablespoons canned bamboo
**   shoots, finely chopped**
1 small (50g) bok choy,
**   finely shredded**
300g uncooked medium prawns,
**   shelled, finely chopped**

Heat oil in small pan, add shallots, ginger, carrot, coriander and bamboo shoots, cook, stirring, about 2 minutes or until carrot is tender. Add bok choy, cook, stirring, until just wilted; cool. Combine prawns with vegetable mixture; mix well.

BEAN CURD AND MUSHROOM
3 Chinese dried mushrooms
2 teaspoons peanut oil
1 green shallot, finely chopped
1/2 teaspoon grated fresh ginger
10 (55g) canned straw mushrooms,
**   finely chopped**
1/4 cup (40g) canned drained baby
**   corn, finely chopped**
1/4 cup (40g) canned drained water
**   chestnuts, finely chopped**
50g firm bean curd (tofu), drained,
**   finely chopped**
1/2 teaspoon sugar

Place mushrooms in small heatproof bowl, cover with boiling water, stand 20 minutes. Drain mushrooms, discard stems, chop caps finely. Heat oil in pan, add all ingredients, cook, stirring, about 3 minutes; cool.

PORK AND CABBAGE
2 teaspoons peanut oil
1 clove garlic, crushed
2 teaspoons grated fresh ginger
2 teaspoons cornflour
1/4 cup (60ml) water
1 tablespoon light soy sauce
4 (125g) Chinese cabbage leaves,
**   finely shredded**
250g minced pork

Heat oil in pan, add garlic and ginger, cook, stirring, until fragrant. Add blended cornflour and water, and sauce, stir over heat until mixture boils and thickens. Add cabbage, cook, stirring, until just wilted; cool. Combine vegetable mixture with pork; mix well.

CHICKEN AND PEANUT
2 Chinese dried mushrooms
1 tablespoon dried shrimp
1/2 stick (55g) celery, finely chopped
1 tablespoon finely chopped
**   unsalted roasted peanuts**
1 clove garlic, crushed
1 green shallot, finely chopped
1 teaspoon hoisin sauce
150g minced chicken

Place mushrooms and shrimp in separate small heatproof bowls, cover with boiling water, stand 20 minutes; drain. Discard stems from mushrooms, chop caps finely. Chop shrimp finely. Combine mushrooms and shrimp in bowl with remaining ingredients; mix well.

DIPPING SAUCES

HONEY CORIANDER SAUCE
1 tablespoon honey
1/2 teaspoon sesame oil
1/4 cup (60ml) chicken stock
2 teaspoons chopped fresh
**   coriander leaves**
1/2 small fresh red chilli,
**   finely chopped**

Combine all ingredients in small bowl; mix well.

BLACK BEAN SAUCE
1 tablespoon black bean sauce
pinch five spice powder
1/3 cup (80ml) chicken stock
2 teaspoons sugar
1/4 teaspoon sesame oil
2 green shallots, finely chopped

Combine all ingredients in small bowl; mix well.

CHICKEN AND PRAWNS ON ASPARAGUS

2 (200g) chicken thigh fillets
12 thick asparagus spears
24 chives
12 (750g) uncooked large prawns
1 tablespoon sesame seeds,
**   toasted**

MARINADE
⅓ cup (80ml) plum sauce
2 tablespoons hoisin sauce
1 tablespoon salt-reduced
**   soy sauce**
1 tablespoon Chinese cooking wine
1 tablespoon water

1. Using a meat mallet, pound chicken fillets gently between layers of plastic wrap until about 3mm thick. Cut each fillet widthways into 6 strips.

3. Drop chives into pan of boiling water, drain immediately, rinse under cold water, drain.

6. Place asparagus in large shallow dish, pour over marinade, cover, refrigerate at least 3 hours. Transfer asparagus to bamboo steamer, cook, covered, over wok or pan of simmering water about 5 minutes or until chicken and prawns are tender.

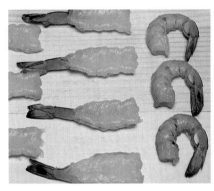

4. Shell prawns, leaving tails intact. Cut prawns along back, cutting nearly all the way through. Remove veins, flatten prawns.

2. Snap off and discard tough ends from asparagus.

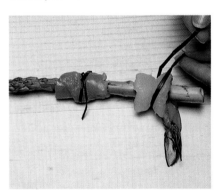

5. Wrap a chicken strip around one end of an asparagus spear, tie with a chive. Wrap a prawn around other end of asparagus spear, tie with a chive. Repeat with remaining chicken, asparagus, prawns and chives.

7. Add marinade to small pan, bring to boil, simmer 1 minute. Drizzle marinade over asparagus, serve sprinkled with seeds.
Marinade: Combine all ingredients in bowl; mix well.

Makes 12.
■ Best cooked just before serving.
■ Freeze: Not suitable.
■ Microwave: Suitable.

Plates and setting from Made in Japan

Lacquered square plate and glass plate from Made in Japan

SCALLOPS WITH BLACK BEAN SAUCE

1 tablespoon packaged salted
   black beans
2 teaspoons peanut oil
1 teaspoon finely chopped
   fresh ginger
½ small fresh red chilli,
   finely chopped
1 clove garlic, crushed
1 tablespoon dry sherry
3 teaspoons dark soy sauce
1 tablespoon rice vinegar
¼ cup (60ml) chicken stock
1 teaspoon sugar
12 uncooked scallops in half shell
2 green shallots, sliced
1 tablespoon chopped fresh
   coriander leaves

1. Rinse, drain and mash black beans. Heat oil in wok or large pan, add ginger, chilli, garlic and black beans, stir-fry until fragrant. Add combined sherry, sauce, vinegar, stock and sugar, simmer, uncovered, about 2 minutes or until slightly thickened.

2. Place scallops in single layer in bamboo steamer, cook, covered, over wok or pan of simmering water a few minutes or until scallops are just opaque. Divide black bean sauce among scallops, top with shallots and coriander.

Makes 12.
■ Best made just before serving.
■ Freeze: Not suitable.
■ Microwave: Scallops suitable.

CRISPY LAYERED FISH

We used ling fillets about 2cm thick in this recipe.

1kg thick white fish fillets
4 green shallots, finely chopped
2 egg whites, lightly beaten
1/3 cup (50g) sesame seeds
1/4 cup (35g) cornflour
1/2 teaspoon sesame oil
1/4 cup (35g) plain flour
1/4 cup (35g) cornflour, extra
1/4 cup (35g) sesame seeds, extra
vegetable oil for deep-frying

CHILLI DIPPING SAUCE
1 small fresh red chilli,
   finely chopped
2 teaspoons finely grated
   fresh ginger
1 clove garlic, crushed
1/4 cup (55g) sugar
2 tablespoons salt-reduced
   soy sauce
1/4 cup (60ml) rice vinegar
1 tablespoon cornflour
1/2 cup (125ml) water

3. Combine flour, extra cornflour and extra seeds in small bowl. Coat fish squares in seed mixture. Heat vegetable oil in wok or large pan, lower fish squares into hot oil, using a slotted spoon, deep-fry until browned and cooked through; drain on absorbent paper. Serve with chilli dipping sauce.

4. **Chilli Dipping Sauce:** Place chilli, ginger and garlic in small pan, stir over heat 1 minute. Add sugar, sauce, vinegar and blended cornflour and water, stir over heat until mixture boils and thickens; cool.

Makes about 35.

■ Best made just before serving. Chilli dipping sauce can be made a day ahead.
■ Storage: Covered, in refrigerator.
■ Microwave: Sauce suitable.

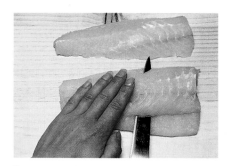

1. Starting from thick end, split fillets horizontally into 3 thin layers, using a sawing motion. Remove any bones.

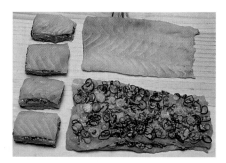

2. Combine shallots, egg whites, seeds, cornflour and sesame oil in bowl, mix to a paste. Spread 1 layer of the fish with some of the paste, top with another layer of fish, then more paste and another layer of fish. Cut into 5cm squares. Repeat with remaining fish and paste.

PRAWN AND CHICKEN ROLLS

Rice noodle sheets should be very fresh and pliable; we used the unrefrigerated variety. If preferred, a 450g plain fresh rice roll can be cut to size.

4 Chinese dried mushrooms
250g uncooked medium prawns
2 teaspoons peanut oil
2 cloves garlic, crushed
2 teaspoons finely grated fresh ginger
4 green shallots, finely chopped
500g minced chicken
¼ cup (30g) canned drained bamboo shoots, finely chopped
1 tablespoon hoisin sauce
1 tablespoon oyster sauce
2 teaspoons cornflour
¼ cup (60ml) chicken stock
1 bunch (about 450g) choy sum
12 fresh rice noodle sheets
1 small (70g) carrot, finely sliced
1 small (150g) yellow pepper, finely sliced
1 small (150g) red pepper, finely sliced

SAUCE
2 tablespoons rice wine
2 tablespoons light soy sauce
¼ teaspoon sugar
¼ cup (60ml) water
2 teaspoons cornflour
1 tablespoon black bean sauce

1. Place mushrooms in heatproof bowl, cover with boiling water, stand 20 minutes. Drain mushrooms, discard stems, chop mushroom caps finely. Shell and devein prawns, process until finely chopped.

2. Heat oil in wok or large pan, add garlic, ginger and shallots, stir-fry until fragrant. Add chicken, stir-fry until browned. Add prawns, mushrooms, bamboo shoots, sauces and blended cornflour and stock; stir-fry until mixture boils and thickens; cool.

3. Cut away and discard choy sum stems. Drop leaves into pan of boiling water, drain immediately, rinse gently under cold water, drain; pat dry with absorbent paper.

4. Cut noodle sheets into 12 rectangles measuring 12cm x 20cm. Top each rectangle with 2 choy sum leaves. Place rounded tablespoons of chicken mixture onto leaves. Fold bottom half of rectangle up, roll sheet over to enclose filling.

5. Place rolls in single layer about 2cm apart in bamboo steamer lined with baking paper. Cook, covered, over wok or pan of simmering water about 6 minutes or until rolls are heated through. Serve rolls with carrot and peppers, drizzled with sauce.

6. Sauce: Combine all ingredients in small pan, stir over heat until mixture boils and thickens slightly.

Makes 12.
■ Best made just before serving.
■ Freeze: Filling suitable.
■ Microwave: Sauce suitable.

Plate from Made in Japan

CRUNCHY SEAFOOD BALLS

12 slices (355g) white bread
500g uncooked medium prawns,
   shelled, deveined
250g squid tubes, chopped
1/2 teaspoon Szechuan seasoning
1/2 teaspoon salt
1/4 cup chopped fresh coriander
   leaves
vegetable oil for deep-frying

DIPPING SAUCE
1/4 cup (60ml) unsweetened
   pineapple juice
1/4 cup (60ml) water
1/4 cup (60ml) tomato sauce
2 tablespoons salt-reduced
   soy sauce
1 tablespoon dry sherry
2 teaspoons white vinegar
1 1/2 teaspoons sugar
1/2 teaspoon grated fresh ginger
1/4 teaspoon chilli oil
1 teaspoon cornflour
2 teaspoons water, extra

1. Cut crusts from bread, place bread on wire racks in single layer, stand several hours or overnight to allow bread to become stale. Cut bread into tiny cubes, place cubes in large bowl.

2. Process prawns, squid, seasoning and salt until almost smooth; stir in coriander. Roll rounded teaspoons of prawn mixture into balls, roll gently in bread cubes.

3. Deep-fry seafood balls in hot oil until browned and cooked through; drain on absorbent paper. Serve with dipping sauce.

4. **Dipping Sauce:** Combine juice, water, sauces, sherry, vinegar, sugar, ginger and oil in small pan. Stir in blended cornflour and extra water, stir over heat until mixture boils and thickens slightly.

Makes about 30.
- Prawn mixture best made just before serving. Dipping sauce can be made a day ahead.
- Storage: Covered, in refrigerator.
- Freeze: Not suitable.
- Microwave: Dipping sauce suitable.

Plate from The Bay Tree Kitchen Shop

Glazed Chilli Ginger Chicken Wings

1.2kg chicken wings
vegetable oil for shallow-frying
1 tablespoon peanut oil
3 cloves garlic, crushed
2cm piece fresh ginger,
**   peeled, sliced**
4 small fresh red chillies, sliced
1 teaspoon chilli powder
1 teaspoon freshly cracked
**   black peppercorns**
2 tablespoons sugar
¼ cup (60ml) chicken stock
¼ cup (60ml) salt-reduced
**   soy sauce**
2 tablespoons oyster sauce
2 tablespoons plum sauce
1 tablespoon rice vinegar
2 teaspoons grated lime rind
¼ teaspoon sesame oil

1. Remove and discard tips from wings. Cut remaining pieces into 2 sections at joint. Place wings in large pan, cover with cold water, bring to boil, simmer, uncovered, 3 minutes. Drain wings, pat dry with absorbent paper.

2. Shallow-fry wings in batches in hot vegetable oil until browned; drain on absorbent paper.

3. Heat peanut oil in wok or pan, add garlic and ginger, stir-fry until fragrant, add chillies, chilli powder, pepper and sugar. Stir in stock, sauces, vinegar, rind and sesame oil. Bring to boil, add wings, cook, stirring, a few minutes or until wings are glazed and heated through.

Makes about 28.

■ Best made just before serving.
■ Freeze: Not suitable.
■ Microwave: Not suitable.

DEEP-FRIED SPRING ROLLS AND DIM SIMS

■ *These golden, fried pastries are among the most popular Chinese savouries you could offer. We made 5 different fillings; each is enough for 24 spring rolls or 48 dim dims. We show you how to shape the dim sims 2 ways.*

■ *Both seafood fillings are best made about 2 hours ahead. If desired, the chicken, beef and vegetarian fillings can be made a day ahead, then covered and refrigerated. All are deep-fried just before serving. None is suitable to freeze or microwave. Dipping sauces can be made a day ahead, covered and refrigerated.*

SPRING ROLLS

24 x 125mm square spring
   roll wrappers
1 egg, lightly beaten
vegetable oil for deep-frying

1. Drop tablespoons of filling across corners of wrappers. Brush edges with a little egg, tuck in ends, roll up to enclose filling.

2. Deep-fry spring rolls in batches in hot oil until golden brown and cooked through; drain on absorbent paper.

DIM SIMS

48 x 125mm square spring
   roll wrappers
1 egg, lightly beaten
vegetable oil for deep-frying

1. **Pouches:** Drop rounded teaspoons of filling in centre of wrappers, shape into pouches; pinch to seal.

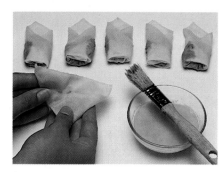

2. **Cloud Swallows:** Drop rounded teaspoons of filling across corners of wrappers. Brush edges with a little egg, fold wrappers up, then fold opposite corners over each other; press to seal. Deep-fry dim sims in batches in hot oil, as for spring rolls, until golden brown and cooked through; drain on absorbent paper.

FILLINGS

PORK AND PRAWN
4 Chinese dried mushrooms
250g uncooked prawns, shelled,
   finely chopped
150g minced pork
3 Chinese cabbage leaves,
   finely shredded
2 teaspoons peanut oil
1 clove garlic, crushed
2 teaspoons finely grated
   fresh ginger
1 small (70g) carrot, finely grated
2 teaspoons finely chopped fresh
   coriander leaves
2 teaspoons finely chopped
   lemon grass
1 tablespoon dark soy sauce
1 tablespoon oyster sauce

Place mushrooms in heatproof bowl, cover with boiling water, stand 20 minutes. Drain mushrooms; discard stems, chop caps finely. Combine with remaining ingredients in bowl; mix well.

FIVE SPICE CHICKEN
4 Chinese dried mushrooms
325g minced chicken
½ cup (100g) canned drained baby
   corn spears, finely chopped
1 tablespoon light soy sauce
¼ teaspoon sesame oil
2 green shallots, finely chopped
½ teaspoon five spice powder
1 teaspoon finely grated
   fresh ginger

Place mushrooms in heatproof bowl, cover with boiling water, stand 20 minutes. Drain mushrooms; discard stems, chop caps finely. Combine mushrooms with remaining ingredients in bowl; mix well.

CRAB AND GINGER
30g bean thread vermicelli noodles
225g cooked or canned crab meat
125g boneless white fish fillets,
   finely chopped
2 teaspoons cornflour
2 teaspoons finely grated fresh ginger
4 green shallots, finely chopped
2 teaspoons dark soy sauce
2 teaspoons oyster sauce

Place noodles in heatproof bowl, cover with boiling water, stand 5 minutes, drain; chop noodles into small pieces. Combine noodles with remaining ingredients in bowl; mix well.

BEAN CURD AND VEGETABLE
4 Chinese dried mushrooms
2 teaspoons peanut oil
2 cloves garlic, crushed
1 tablespoon finely grated
fresh ginger
4 green shallots, finely chopped
80g oyster mushrooms,
finely chopped
100g packaged fried bean curd,
finely chopped
1 medium (120g) carrot,
finely grated
3 Chinese cabbage leaves,
finely shredded
1 teaspoon cornflour
2 teaspoons dark soy sauce
1 teaspoon oyster sauce

Place dried mushrooms in heatproof bowl, cover with boiling water, stand 20 minutes. Drain mushrooms; discard stems, chop caps finely. Heat oil in wok, add garlic, ginger and shallots, cook, stirring, until fragrant. Add all mushrooms, bean curd and carrot, stir-fry 1 minute; remove from heat. Stir in cabbage, cornflour and sauces; mix well; cool.

BEEF AND CABBAGE
4 Chinese dried mushrooms
300g minced beef
6 canned drained water chestnuts,
finely chopped
2 Chinese cabbage leaves,
finely shredded
½ small (40g) onion, finely chopped
1 teaspoon finely grated
fresh ginger
2 teaspoons dark soy sauce
2 teaspoons cornflour
1 tablespoon water
½ teaspoon chilli oil

Place mushrooms in heatproof bowl, cover with boiling water, stand 20 minutes. Drain mushrooms; discard stems, chop caps finely. Combine mushrooms with remaining ingredients in bowl; mix well.

DIPPING SAUCES

CHILLI GINGER SAUCE
⅓ cup (80ml) chicken stock
2 teaspoons finely grated
fresh ginger
1 tablespoon dried crushed chillies
2 tablespoons dark soy sauce
2 teaspoons Chinese cooking wine
2 tablespoons chopped fresh
coriander leaves

Combine all ingredients in small bowl; mix well.

PLUM SESAME SAUCE
½ cup (125ml) plum sauce
1 teaspoon sesame oil
⅓ cup (80ml) chicken stock

Combine all ingredients in small bowl; mix well.

Clockwise from top: Dim Sim Pouches; Spring Rolls; Dim Sim Cloud Swallows. Dipping Sauces from left: Plum Sesame; Chilli Ginger.

STEAMED PORK BUNS

1½ teaspoons (10g) dry yeast
¼ cup (55g) caster sugar
1¼ cups (310ml) warm water
3 cups (450g) plain flour
1 teaspoon baking powder

FILLING
2 Chinese dried mushrooms
2 teaspoons peanut oil
1 clove garlic, crushed
1 teaspoon grated fresh ginger
200g Chinese barbecued
   pork, shredded
2 tablespoons salt-reduced
   soy sauce
1 tablespoon hoisin sauce
1 tablespoon oyster sauce
2 teaspoons cornflour
½ cup (125ml) water

1. Mark 12 x 4cm squares on baking paper, spray paper with oil, cut out squares. Combine yeast, 1 tablespoon of the sugar and ¼ cup (60ml) of the water in small bowl, cover, stand in warm place about 15 minutes or until mixture is frothy.

Sift flour and baking powder into large bowl, stir in remaining sugar. Stir in yeast mixture and remaining water, mix to a soft dough. Knead dough on floured surface for about 5 minutes or until dough is smooth and elastic. Place dough in oiled bowl, cover, stand in warm place about 1½ hours or until dough has doubled in size. Turn dough onto floured surface, knead 3 minutes; divide dough into 12 pieces.

2. Roll 1 piece of dough into a 12cm round on floured surface. Using ⅓ cup capacity metric measuring cup, ease dough into cup. Place a slightly rounded tablespoon of filling in centre, press filling down. Dip fingers in water, gather dough together with fingers, twist at top. Place a piece of the oiled paper over join. Repeat with remaining dough and filling.

3. Place buns, paper side down, on baking paper-covered trays, cover, stand in warm place about 30 minutes or until buns are nearly doubled in size.

4. Steam buns on paper squares in batches in large, covered bamboo steamer over wok or pan of simmering water about 20 minutes or until buns are puffed and cooked through.

5. Filling: Place mushrooms in heat-proof bowl, cover with boiling water, stand 20 minutes. Drain mushrooms; discard stems, chop caps finely. Heat oil in wok or pan, add garlic, ginger and mushrooms, stir-fry until fragrant. Add pork, sauces and blended cornflour and water, stir until mixture boils and thickens; cool.
Makes 12.

■ Pork buns must be made just before serving. Filling can be made a day ahead.
■ Storage: Covered, in refrigerator.
■ Freeze: Not suitable.
■ Microwave: Filling suitable.

STEAMED CLAMS WITH CHILLI CREAM FILLING

1kg clams
2 tablespoons coarse cooking salt
1 cup (250ml) water
4cm piece fresh ginger,
    peeled, sliced
2 tablespoons dry sherry
250g boneless white fish fillets
1 green shallot, chopped
1 egg white
2 tablespoons cream
1 teaspoon oyster sauce
½ teaspoon hot chilli sauce
1 small clove garlic, crushed

SAUCE
2 teaspoons cornflour
1 tablespoon dry sherry
⅓ cup (80ml) chicken stock
1 tablespoon lemon juice
1 tablespoon honey
1 tablespoon light soy sauce
1 small fresh red chilli,
    finely chopped

Setting from Made in Japan

1. Scrub clams, place in large bowl, cover with cold water, stir in half the salt, stand 20 minutes. Drain clams. Repeat process, using remaining salt. Rinse clams thoroughly; drain well.

2. Combine the water, ginger and sherry in large shallow pan, bring to boil, add clams, remove with a slotted spoon as soon as the shells open. Discard cooking liquid.

3. Process remaining ingredients until smooth. Press teaspoons of fish filling onto each clam. Place clams in single layer in bamboo steamer, cover, steam over wok or pan of simmering water about 1 minute or until fish filling feels firm to touch. Serve hot clams drizzled with sauce.

4. **Sauce:** Blend cornflour with sherry in small pan, stir in remaining ingredients, cook, stirring, until sauce boils and thickens slightly.
Serves 4 to 6.

■ Best made just before serving.
■ Freeze: Not suitable.
■ Microwave: Not suitable.

PORK AND BROCCOLI PANCAKE BUNDLES

⅓ bunch (165g) Chinese broccoli
1 tablespoon peanut oil
300g minced pork
2 cloves garlic, crushed
¼ cup (60ml) hoisin sauce
16 x 16cm round rice paper sheets
1½ tablespoons plain flour
1½ tablespoons water
¼ bunch (25g) garlic chives,
    roughly chopped
2½ cups (200g) bean sprouts
16 garlic chives, approximately,
    extra

DIPPING SAUCE
2 tablespoons dry sherry
3 teaspoons salt-reduced soy sauce
2 teaspoons sugar
2 teaspoons sambal oelek

1. Trim stems from broccoli, finely shred leaves. Heat oil in wok or large pan, add pork and garlic, stir-fry until pork is browned. Remove from heat, stir in sauce.

2. Place each sheet of rice paper individually into a bowl of warm water for about 1 minute or until slightly softened; gently lift from water, place on board, pat dry with absorbent paper.

3. Blend flour with water until smooth. Brush 8 of the rice paper sheets all over with flour mixture, top with pork mixture, then chopped chives, broccoli and sprouts. Place remaining sheets over vegetables, press sheets together to seal.

4. Drop extra chives into pan of boiling water, drain immediately, rinse under cold water; drain. Gently roll up rice paper parcels, secure with 2 chives tied together; trim ends with scissors.

5. Place bundles in single layer in bamboo steamer lined with baking paper, cook, covered, over wok or pan of simmering water about 10 minutes or until heated through. Serve with dipping sauce.
Dipping Sauce: Combine all ingredients in bowl; mix well.
Makes 8.

■ Best made just before serving.
■ Freeze: Not suitable.
■ Microwave: Not suitable.

Setting from Made in Japan

POULTRY

Mouth-watering chicken and duck dishes are a popular part of Chinese cooking and you'll quickly appreciate why when you sample our wonderful recipes. The flavours are subtle and fresh, with lots of interesting tastes based on favourite dishes from many different regions. For a special occasion or dinner party, enjoy our version of Peking Duck, one of China's most famous specialties.

GARLIC GINGER CHICKEN IN BOK CHOY

6 Chinese dried mushrooms
8 green shallots
6 (660g) baby bok choy
2 tablespoons peanut oil
2 cloves garlic, crushed
2 teaspoons grated fresh ginger
450g minced chicken
1 tablespoon dark soy sauce
1 tablespoon light soy sauce
1 tablespoon Chinese cooking wine
1/3 cup (80ml) chicken stock
1 tablespoon cornflour
1 tablespoon water

2. Carefully cut each bok choy lengthways through leaves and stems, cutting about three-quarters of the way through. Gently open bok choy to form a "V" shape.

4. Divide filling among bok choy to within about 7cm of the ends of the leaves. Tie bok choy with string about 7cm from ends of leaves. Tie a shallot around centre, trim ends.

1. Place mushrooms in small heatproof bowl, cover with boiling water, stand 20 minutes. Drain mushrooms, discard stems, slice caps thinly. Finely slice 2 of the shallots. Drop remaining shallots into pan of boiling water, remove from heat, stand 2 minutes or until soft, drain, rinse under cold water, drain.

3. Heat oil in wok or large pan, add garlic and ginger, stir-fry until fragrant. Add chicken, stir-fry until chicken is browned and tender. Add mushrooms, sliced shallots, sauces, wine, stock and blended cornflour and water, stir until mixture boils and thickens. Cool mixture 5 minutes.

5. Place bok choy in single layer in bamboo steamer over wok or pan of simmering water, steam, covered, about 5 minutes or until bok choy are tender.
Makes 6.

■ Best made just before serving.
■ Freeze: Not suitable.
■ Microwave: Filled bok choy suitable.

BRAISED CHICKEN ON CRISP NOODLES

12 (20g) Chinese dried mushrooms
2 tablespoons peanut oil
700g chicken thigh fillets,
    thinly sliced
1 bunch (600g) spring
    onions, quartered
3 cloves garlic, crushed
2 teaspoons grated fresh ginger
1 medium (200g) red pepper, sliced
1 bunch (340g) baby bok
    choy, chopped
1 teaspoon sugar
1 tablespoon oyster sauce
2 tablespoons light soy sauce
2 teaspoons cornflour
¼ cup (60ml) water
500g packet hokkien noodles
vegetable oil for deep-frying
2 tablespoons chopped fresh chives

2. Heat half the peanut oil in wok or large pan, add chicken in batches, stir-fry until chicken is browned and tender, remove from wok. Heat remaining peanut oil in wok, add onions, garlic, ginger and pepper, stir-fry until onions are soft and lightly browned.

4. Deep-fry noodles in hot vegetable oil in batches until golden and crisp; drain on absorbent paper. Serve chicken and vegetables on noodles, sprinkled with chives.
Serves 4.

■ Best made just before serving.
■ Freeze: Not suitable.
■ Microwave: Not suitable.

1. Place mushrooms in heatproof bowl, cover with boiling water, stand 20 minutes. Drain mushrooms, discard stems, slice caps.

3. Add chicken, mushrooms, bok choy, sugar and sauces to wok, stir in blended cornflour and water, stir over heat until mixture boils and thickens.

CHICKEN AND VEGETABLES WITH BLACK BEAN SAUCE

1kg chicken breast fillets, sliced
1 teaspoon sesame oil
1 teaspoon grated fresh ginger
2 cloves garlic, crushed
¼ cup (40g) packaged salted
**   black beans**
¼ cup (60ml) peanut oil
2 medium (300g) onions, sliced
1 large (180g) carrot, sliced
1 medium (200g) red pepper, sliced
125g fresh baby corn
100g broccoli florets
⅓ cup (80ml) chicken stock
2 tablespoons thick dark soy sauce
2 tablespoons chilli sauce
2 teaspoons sugar
3 teaspoons cornflour
1 tablespoon water
80g snow pea sprouts

1. Combine chicken, sesame oil, ginger and garlic in bowl, mix well, cover, refrigerate 1 hour. Rinse, drain and mash beans. Heat 2 tablespoons of the peanut oil in wok or large pan, add chicken in batches, stir-fry until chicken is tender. Remove, cover to keep warm.

2. Heat remaining peanut oil in wok, add onions, stir-fry until onions are soft. Add carrot, pepper, corn and broccoli, stir-fry until vegetables are just tender. Stir in combined beans, stock, sauces and sugar, then blended cornflour and water, stir over heat until mixture boils

and thickens. Add chicken and sprouts, stir gently until hot.
Serves 6.

■ Chicken can be marinated
    a day ahead.
■ Storage: Covered, in refrigerator.
■ Freeze: Not suitable.
■ Microwave: Not suitable.

CHICKEN AND EGG NOODLE STIR-FRY

350g thin fresh egg noodles
1 tablespoon peanut oil
6 (660g) chicken thigh fillets, sliced
1 teaspoon finely grated
   fresh ginger
1 small fresh red chilli, finely sliced
1 small (80g) onion, sliced
1 medium (120g) carrot, sliced
3 (100g) Chinese sausages, sliced
1 teaspoon peanut oil, extra
4 eggs, lightly beaten
2 teaspoons salt-reduced soy sauce
1 tablespoon oyster sauce
2 teaspoons Chinese cooking wine
1/4 cup (60ml) chicken stock
1/4 teaspoon sesame oil

CRUNCHY SHRIMP TOPPING
4 green shallots, sliced
1 clove garlic, crushed
1/4 cup (30g) dried shrimp, chopped

1. Add noodles to large pan of boiling water, boil about 1 minute or until noodles rise to surface, drain; rinse under cold water, drain well.

2. Heat half the peanut oil in wok or large pan, add chicken in batches, stir-fry until chicken is browned and tender; remove. Heat remaining peanut oil in wok, add ginger, chilli, onion, carrot and sausages, stir-fry until carrot is just tender; remove.

3. Heat half the extra peanut oil in wok, add half the eggs, swirl wok so eggs form a thin omelette over base, cook until set, remove, cool. Repeat with remaining extra peanut oil and eggs. Roll omelettes firmly, cut into thin slices.

4. Return chicken to wok with vegetable mixture, omelette slices, noodles and remaining ingredients, stir-fry until heated through. Serve sprinkled with crunchy shrimp topping.

5. **Crunchy Shrimp Topping:** Add shallots, garlic and shrimp to wok, stir-fry until heated through.
Serves 4 to 6.

■ Best just made before serving.
■ Freeze: Not suitable.
■ Microwave: Not suitable.

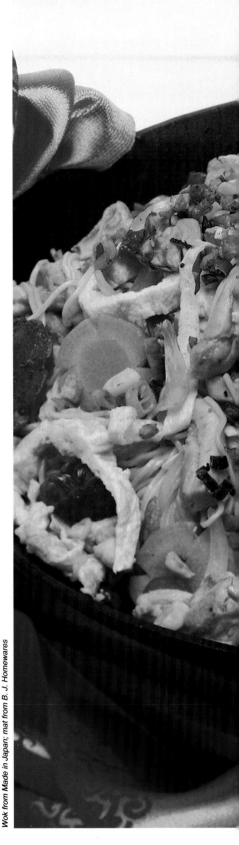

Wok from Made in Japan; mat from B. J. Homewares

PEKING DUCK WITH PANCAKES

We used the more fleshy Muscovy duck in this recipe.

2kg duck
1/4 cup (60ml) honey, warmed
1 small (160g) Lebanese cucumber
8 green shallots

PANCAKES
1½ cups (225g) plain flour
1½ teaspoons sugar
3/4 cup (180ml) boiling water

SAUCE
1/3 cup (80ml) hoisin sauce
2 tablespoons chicken stock
1 tablespoon plum sauce

1. Wash duck, drain well. Tie string around neck of duck. Lower duck into large pan of boiling water for 20 seconds, remove from pan, drain well; pat dry with absorbent paper. Tie string to a refrigerator shelf and suspend duck, uncovered, over drip tray overnight. Remove duck from refrigerator, suspend duck in front of cold air from an electric fan about 2 hours or until skin is dry to the touch.

2. Tuck wings under duck. Place duck breast side up on wire rack in large baking dish, brush entire duck evenly with honey. Bake, uncovered, in moderate oven 30 minutes, turn duck, reduce heat to slow, bake, uncovered, about 1 hour or until tender.

3. Place duck on chopping board, remove skin, place skin in single layer on wire rack over oven tray. Bake skin, uncovered, in moderate oven about 10 minutes or until crisp and browned; slice skin. Slice duck meat. Remove cucumber seeds. Cut cucumber and shallots into thin 8cm strips. To serve, top warm pancakes with duck meat, crisp skin, cucumber, shallots and sauce, roll, eat with fingers.

4. **Pancakes:** Sift flour and sugar into large bowl, add water, stir quickly with wooden spoon until ingredients cling together. Knead dough on floured surface about 10 minutes or until smooth. Wrap dough in plastic wrap, stand 30 minutes at room temperature.

5. Divide dough into 16 pieces. Roll a piece into a 16cm round. Heat small heavy-based frying pan, dry-fry pancake about 10 seconds on each side or until very lightly browned. Repeat with remaining dough. Wrap cooked pancakes in foil as they are cooked to prevent drying out. If necessary, pan-

cakes can be reheated in a bamboo steamer or microwave oven.

Line steamer with a cloth, place pancakes in single layer on cloth, steam over simmering water about 2 minutes or until pancakes are heated through.

Setting from Made in Japan

Sauce: Combine all ingredients in small bowl, mix well. Serves 4.

■ Duck must be prepared a day ahead.
■ Storage: Uncovered, in refrigerator.
■ Freeze: Not suitable.
■ Microwave: Not suitable.

QUICK 'N' EASY SATÉ CHICKEN

We used a Chinese-style saté sauce.

750g chicken thigh fillets
2 teaspoons peanut oil
3 medium (450g) onions, chopped
3/4 cup (180ml) bottled saté sauce
1 clove garlic, crushed
1/4 cup (60ml) chicken stock
2 green shallots, thinly sliced

2. Add onions to wok, stir-fry until onions are soft.

3. Stir in chicken, sauce, garlic and stock, stir until heated through. Serve sprinkled with shallots.
Serves 4.

■ Best made just before serving.
■ Freeze: Not suitable.
■ Microwave: Not suitable.

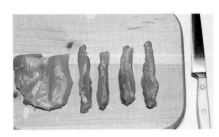

1. Cut chicken into thin strips. Heat oil in wok or large pan, add chicken in batches, stir-fry until chicken is tender; remove from wok.

CHICKEN RICE WITH SOUP

This dish comprises chicken and rice with soup and vegetables, plus accompaniments such as sliced chillies and shallots, grated ginger, chopped garlic and sauce for dipping. The soup is eaten along with the hot chicken, rice and accompaniments.

1.9kg chicken
2 litres (8 cups) water
2 small (400g) leeks, chopped
2 sticks celery, chopped
2cm piece fresh ginger,
  peeled, sliced
1 star anise
1 tablespoon sesame oil
1 tablespoon peanut oil
1 medium (150g) onion, chopped
2 cloves garlic, crushed
1 tablespoon grated fresh
  ginger, extra
1½ cups (300g) jasmine rice
1 small (70g) carrot, sliced
80g broccoli florets
80g snow peas, halved
2 tablespoons salt-reduced
  soy sauce
fresh coriander leaves

SAUCE
2 tablespoons salt-reduced
  soy sauce
1 tablespoon rice vinegar
1 tablespoon water
1 teaspoon sesame oil

1. Chop chicken into bite-sized pieces. Combine chicken, water, leeks, celery, ginger and star anise in large pan, simmer, covered, about 20 minutes or until chicken is tender; skim occasionally.

2. Remove chicken to plate, brush with half the sesame oil, cover to keep warm. Strain stock through fine sieve, discard pulp.

3. Heat peanut oil and remaining sesame oil in large pan, add onion, garlic and extra ginger, stir-fry until onion is soft. Add rice, stir until grains are well coated in oil mixture. Stir in 2½ cups (625ml) of the stock, cover tightly, bring to boil, reduce heat to as low as possible, cook 15 minutes. Do not remove lid during cooking time. Remove from heat, stand, covered, 10 minutes.

Meanwhile, boil, steam or microwave carrot, broccoli and snow peas until just tender. Return remaining stock to clean pan, stir in soy sauce, bring soup to boil. Place a few coriander leaves in each serving bowl and top with soup.
Sauce: Combine all ingredients in small bowl; mix well.
Serves 6.

- Best made close to serving.
- Freeze: Cooked chicken and stock suitable.
- Microwave: Vegetables suitable.

CHILLI CHICKEN STIR-FRY

1 tablespoon mild sweet chilli sauce
2 tablespoons hoisin sauce
2 tablespoons salt-reduced
    soy sauce
2 tablespoons honey
2 tablespoons rice vinegar
3 cloves garlic, crushed
1 teaspoon grated fresh ginger
3 small fresh red chillies, sliced
800g chicken thigh fillets, quartered
2 large (400g) onions
2 bunches (500g) asparagus
2 tablespoons peanut oil
1 bunch (340g) baby bok choy,
    shredded

1. Combine sauces, honey, vinegar, garlic, ginger and chillies in large bowl, add chicken, mix well. Cover; refrigerate 3 hours or overnight.

2. Halve onions, cut into wedges. Snap off and discard tough ends of asparagus; cut asparagus into 4cm pieces. Boil, steam or microwave asparagus until just tender, rinse under cold water, drain.

3. Drain chicken from marinade, reserve marinade. Heat half the oil in wok or large pan, add onions, stir-fry until onions are soft, remove. Heat remaining oil in wok, add chicken, stir-fry until lightly browned. Add marinade, bring to boil, cover, simmer about 10 minutes or until chicken is tender, stirring occasionally. Add onions, asparagus and bok choy, cook, stirring, until bok choy is just wilted.
Serves 4 to 6.

■ Best made just before serving.
■ Freeze: Not suitable.
■ Microwave: Asparagus suitable.

Plate, mat and box from Storehouse

Mat, spoon and fork from Home & Garden on the Mall; fan from Eastern Flair; fabric from St James

CHINESE CHICKEN SALAD

8 (880g) chicken thigh fillets
1 teaspoon salt
2 teaspoons coarsely ground
  black peppercorns
1/2 teaspoon five spice powder
4 Chinese dried mushrooms
1 bunch (380g) Chinese broccoli
2 sticks celery, sliced
4 green shallots, sliced
1 1/4 cups (100g) bean sprouts
1 medium carrot, sliced
425g can baby corn spears,
  drained, halved

DRESSING
2 tablespoons salt-reduced
  soy sauce
1 tablespoon peanut oil
1/4 cup (60ml) chicken stock
3 teaspoons rice vinegar
1 teaspoon finely grated
  fresh ginger
1 clove garlic, crushed
1 small fresh red chilli, thinly sliced

1. Place chicken in single layer on wire rack on oven tray. Sprinkle 1 side of chicken with half the combined salt, pepper and spice. Place under hot grill, cook until browned and crisp. Turn chicken, sprinkle with remaining spice mixture, grill until chicken is tender; cool. Cut chicken into pieces.

2. Meanwhile, place mushrooms in heatproof bowl, cover with boiling water, stand 20 minutes. Discard stems, slice caps finely. Cut leaves from broccoli stems, drop leaves and stems into pan of boiling water for 1 minute; drain, rinse under cold water, drain well. Combine chicken, mushrooms, broccoli, celery, shallots, sprouts, carrot and corn in large bowl with dressing; mix well.
Dressing: Combine all ingredients in jar; shake well.
Serves 4 to 6.

■ Best made close to serving.
■ Freeze: Not suitable.
■ Microwave: Not suitable.

BEEF, LAMB & PORK

Stir up some appreciation with these delicious meat dishes! Pork is a favourite in China and we show you some of the myriad of ways it can be prepared. Beef, too, is popular and its taste and texture are perfectly complemented by stronger flavourings. There are fewer lamb dishes in China but included in this section is our special Mongolian lamb stir-fry.

MARINATED BEEF WITH SPICY BARBECUE SAUCE

**800g piece beef eye-fillet,
  thinly sliced**
2 cloves garlic, crushed
3 small fresh red chillies, chopped
2 bunches (500g) asparagus
250g fresh baby corn, halved
2 tablespoons peanut oil
**1 large (350g) red pepper,
  thinly sliced**
2 tablespoons plum sauce
**¼ cup (60ml) Chinese
  barbecue sauce**
2 teaspoons rice vinegar
2 tablespoons tomato paste

1. Combine beef, garlic and chillies in bowl; mix well. Cover, refrigerate 3 hours or overnight.

2. Snap off and discard tough ends from asparagus; cut asparagus into 4cm pieces. Add asparagus and corn to pan of boiling water, boil, uncovered, 1 minute, drain, rinse under cold water; drain well.

3. Heat oil in wok or large pan, add beef mixture in batches, stir-fry until beef is browned and tender. Return beef to wok with asparagus and corn, pepper and combined sauces, vinegar and paste, stir-fry until mixture boils. Serves 6.

■ Best made just before serving.
■ Freeze: Not suitable.
■ Microwave: Asparagus and corn suitable.

Tray from Morris Home & Garden Wares

CANTONESE ROAST DUCK

We used the more fleshy Muscovy duck in this recipe.

1.8kg duck
1 teaspoon coarse cooking salt
1 tablespoon cornflour
³/4 cup (180ml) water

LIQUID SEASONING
3 cloves garlic, crushed
2 star anise
2 tablespoons thick soy sauce
2 tablespoons soy bean paste
2 tablespoons dry sherry
1 tablespoon brown sugar
1 tablespoon honey
2 teaspoons grated fresh ginger
1 teaspoon Szechuan pepper
1/2 teaspoon salt

GLAZE
2 tablespoons honey
2 tablespoons white vinegar
2 teaspoons thick soy sauce
2 tablespoons boiling water

3. Place duck breast side up on wire rack in baking dish. Bake, uncovered, in moderately hot oven 30 minutes. Baste duck all over with glaze, cover wing and leg tips with foil, turn duck, reduce heat to moderate, bake 30 minutes. Baste again with glaze, turn duck, reduce heat to moderately slow, bake about 25 minutes or until duck is tender and skin crisp. Remove toothpicks or thread. Chop duck into bite-sized portions. Cover to keep warm.

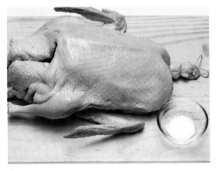

1. Rinse duck cavity with cold water; pat dry inside and out with absorbent paper. Rub duck inside and out with salt. Tie neck tightly with string. Tie duck to a refrigerator shelf and suspend duck, uncovered, over drip tray for 1 hour.

4. Strain seasoning from duck into small pan, stir in blended cornflour and water, stir over heat until mixture boils and thickens. Serve sauce with duck.
Liquid Seasoning: Combine all ingredients in bowl; mix well.
Glaze: Combine all ingredients in bowl; mix well.
Serves 4.

■ Best made close to serving.
■ Freeze: Not suitable.
■ Microwave: Not suitable.

2. Brush inside duck with liquid seasoning, pour remainder of seasoning into duck; secure openings with toothpicks or stitch together.

Setting from Made in Japan

CRISP-SKINNED DUCK WITH PLUM SAUCE

2 tablespoons cornflour
1 teaspoon five spice powder
6 (1kg) duck breast fillets

PLUM SAUCE
825g can whole plums in natural
    juice, drained, chopped
¼ cup (60ml) water
1 tablespoon rice vinegar
¼ cup (55g) sugar
1 teaspoon cornflour
2 teaspoons water, extra

1. Combine cornflour and spice in large bowl. Toss fillets in mixture to coat evenly. Prick skin all over with the point of a sharp knife.

2. Place fillets skin side up in single layer on oven tray, cook under slow grill until fillets slowly cook through, increase heat to high, cook until skin becomes crisp. Drain on absorbent paper. Serve with plum sauce.

3. **Plum Sauce:** Combine plums, water, vinegar and sugar in small pan, stir over heat until sugar is dissolved. Simmer, uncovered, without stirring, about 15 minutes or until plums are pulpy. Stir in blended cornflour and extra water, stir until mixture boils and thickens slightly.
Serves 4 to 6.

■ Best made just before serving.
■ Freeze: Not suitable.
■ Microwave: Plum sauce suitable.

CHINESE ROAST PORK OMELETTES

800g pork fillets
2 tablespoons salt-reduced
  soy sauce
1 tablespoon oyster sauce
2 tablespoons honey
2 tablespoons dry sherry
2 green shallots, sliced

OMELETTES
10 eggs
¼ cup (60ml) water
1 tablespoon salt-reduced
  soy sauce
2 teaspoons Szechuan seasoning
1 clove garlic, crushed
¾ cup (60g) bean sprouts
4 green shallots, finely sliced
2 tablespoons peanut oil,
  approximately

SAUCE
½ cup (125ml) water
1 teaspoon cornflour
1½ tablespoons oyster sauce

1. Place pork in shallow plastic or glass dish, pour over combined sauces, honey and sherry; mix well. Cover dish; refrigerate 3 hours or overnight.

2. Remove pork from marinade; reserve marinade. Place pork on wire rack in baking dish. Bake, uncovered, in hot oven 20 minutes, reduce heat to moderate, bake about 15 minutes or until pork is tender, basting occasionally with some of the reserved marinade. Stand pork 5 minutes, slice thinly, cover to keep warm.

Place an omelette on serving plate, top with pork slices. Repeat layering, ending with an omelette. Pour sauce over omelettes, top with shallots.

3. Omelettes: Whisk eggs, water, sauce, seasoning and garlic together in bowl, add sprouts and shallots.

4. Brush 20cm heavy-based frying-pan with some of the oil, heat pan, pour ⅓ cup (80ml) of the omelette mixture into pan. Cook, uncovered, until set underneath, turn, cook other side. Remove omelette from pan, place on sheet of baking paper. Repeat with remaining oil and omelette mixture, layering cooked omelettes between baking paper.

Sauce: Combine reserved marinade, water and blended cornflour and sauce in pan, stir over heat until mixture boils and thickens slightly.

Serves 6.

■ Omelettes must be made just
  before serving. Pork can be
  prepared a day ahead.
■ Storage: Covered, in refrigerator.
■ Freeze: Not suitable.
■ Microwave: Not suitable.

Bowls and abacus from Made in Japan

BEEF AND SNAKE BEANS WITH NOODLES

250g rice vermicelli noodles
2 teaspoons sesame oil
2 medium (300g) onions, sliced
2 tablespoons red vinegar
1 tablespoon brown sugar
1 tablespoon peanut oil
600g beef eye-fillet, thinly sliced
2 teaspoons grated fresh ginger
3 cloves garlic, crushed
¼ cup (60ml) hoisin sauce
2 tablespoons salt-reduced
**   soy sauce**
2 tablespoons chopped fresh
**   coriander leaves**
250g snake beans, chopped
1 tablespoon sesame seeds

1. Place noodles in heatproof bowl, cover with boiling water, stand 5 minutes, drain.

2. Heat half the sesame oil in wok or large pan, add onions, vinegar and sugar, cook over low heat, stirring occasionally, until onions are caramelised; remove.

3. Heat peanut oil in wok, add beef in batches, stir-fry until browned and tender; remove.

4. Heat remaining sesame oil in wok, add ginger, garlic, sauces, coriander, beans and seeds, stir-fry until beans are just tender. Return beef and onions to wok with noodles, stir until heated through.
Serves 4.

▪ Best made just before serving.
▪ Freeze: Not suitable.
▪ Microwave: Not suitable.

Bowls from Accoutrement; fabric from St James Furnishings

PORK AND EGGPLANT WITH NOODLES

2 tablespoons peanut oil
1 teaspoon sesame oil
4 cloves garlic, crushed
1 tablespoon finely chopped
    fresh ginger
9 (550g) finger eggplants, sliced
¼ cup (60ml) water
1 tablespoon peanut oil, extra
500g minced pork
500g hokkien noodles
¼ cup (60ml) Chinese
    barbecue sauce
¼ cup (60ml) tomato sauce
2 tablespoons hoisin sauce
1 teaspoon hot chilli sauce
1 tablespoon Chinese cooking wine
¼ cup chopped fresh
    coriander leaves

1. Heat peanut and sesame oils in wok or large pan, add garlic and ginger, stir-fry until fragrant. Add eggplants, stir-fry 2 minutes. Add half the water, stir-fry 2 minutes. Add remaining water, stir-fry until eggplants are browned and tender; remove.

2. Heat extra peanut oil in wok, add pork in batches, stir-fry until browned and tender. Return pork to wok. Add noodles, stir-fry until noodles are tender. Add combined sauces, wine and eggplant, stir until heated through. Stir in coriander.
Serves 4 to 6.

■ Best made just before serving.
■ Freeze: Not suitable.
■ Microwave: Not suitable.

Bowls from Made in Japan

SWEET AND SOUR PORK SPARE RIBS

Sometimes pork spare ribs have a long bone that is hard to chop at home; in this case, ask your butcher to prepare the ribs for you.

6 (1kg) pork spare ribs
2 teaspoons peanut oil
2 medium (300g) onions, chopped
100g snow peas, halved
1 small (150g) red pepper, chopped
1¼ cups (200g) chopped
    fresh pineapple
⅓ cup (75g) sugar
¼ cup (60ml) white vinegar
½ cup (125ml) chicken stock
½ cup (125ml) tomato puree
2 teaspoons light soy sauce
2 teaspoons cornflour
1 tablespoon water

MARINADE
⅓ cup (80ml) Chinese
    barbecue sauce
2 tablespoons light soy sauce
1 teaspoon hot chilli sauce
¼ cup (60ml) honey
2 tablespoons brown malt vinegar
2 cloves garlic, crushed

1. Chop ribs into 5cm lengths, combine in large bowl with marinade; mix well. Cover, refrigerate 3 hours or overnight.

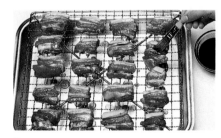

2. Drain ribs, reserve marinade. Place ribs on wire rack over baking dish, brush with reserved marinade. Pour enough water into dish to just cover base. Bake ribs, uncovered, in moderately hot oven about 45 minutes or until ribs are tender; brush with remaining marinade while cooking. Turn ribs once during cooking.

3. Heat oil in wok or large pan, add onions, stir-fry until just soft. Add snow peas, pepper and pineapple, stir-fry until pepper is just soft. Stir in combined sugar, vinegar, stock, puree and sauce, then blended cornflour and water, stir over heat until mixture boils and thickens. Add ribs, stir gently until heated through.
Marinade: Combine all ingredients in bowl; mix well.
Serves 4.

■ Best made just before serving.
■ Freeze: Not suitable.
■ Microwave: Not suitable.

SESAME LAMB SKEWERS

600g lamb fillets
2 teaspoons Szechuan pepper
½ teaspoon salt
2 eggs, lightly beaten
1 clove garlic, crushed
⅓ cup (50g) plain flour
¼ cup (60ml) sesame sauce
2 tablespoons water
1 tablespoon tomato paste
1 tablespoon dry sherry
1 teaspoon finely chopped
   fresh ginger
¼ teaspoon five spice powder
1 teaspoon sugar
1½ tablespoons dried black
   sesame seeds
1 tablespoon white sesame seeds
peanut oil for shallow-frying

3. Combine pepper mixture, eggs, garlic, flour, sauce, water, paste, sherry, ginger, spice and sugar in bowl; whisk until combined. Add lamb; mix well.

1. Cut lamb into 1cm slices.

4. Thread lamb evenly onto about 16 skewers; sprinkle with combined sesame seeds.

2. Heat small heavy-based pan, add pepper and salt, cook, stirring, until pepper browns slightly and starts to smoke; cool. Crush mixture, using blade of large knife or cleaver.

5. Heat oil in large heavy-based pan, shallow-fry skewers in batches, turning occasionally, until lamb is browned and tender. Drain on absorbent paper. Serves 6.

■ Best prepared on day of serving.
■ Storage: Covered, in refrigerator.
■ Freeze: Not suitable.
■ Microwave: Not suitable.

Ch'ing Dynasty figurine from Alexandra McKenzie Interiors; plates from Made in Japan

CHILLI PORK WITH SZECHUAN PICKLES

1.5kg piece boneless pork belly
1 tablespoon peanut oil
1 small (150g) red pepper, sliced
1 small (70g) carrot, sliced
3 cloves garlic, thinly sliced
150g snow pea sprouts
⅓ cup (60g) packaged Szechuan pickles, chopped
4 small fresh red chillies, sliced
1 teaspoon Szechuan pepper, crushed
2 tablespoons salted soya beans in sauce, mashed
2 tablespoons dry sherry
2 tablespoons sweet thick soy sauce
1 tablespoon hoisin sauce
1 teaspoon hot chilli sauce
1 tablespoon sugar
1 teaspoon cornflour
⅓ cup (80ml) water

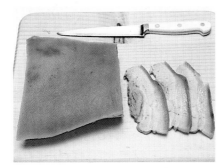

1. Place pork in pan of boiling water, simmer, covered, 25 minutes. Remove from heat, stand, covered, 10 minutes. Drain pork well; slice thinly.

2. Heat half the oil in wok or large pan, add red pepper, carrot and half the garlic, stir-fry until vegetables are almost tender, stir in sprouts; remove, cover to keep warm.

3. Heat remaining oil in wok, add remaining garlic, pickles, chillies and Szechuan pepper, stir-fry until fragrant. Stir in combined beans, sherry, sauces, sugar and blended cornflour and water, stir over heat until mixture boils and thickens. Add pork, mix gently until heated through. Serve pork mixture with vegetables.
Serves 6.

- Best made just before serving.
- Freeze: Not suitable.
- Microwave: Not suitable.

Gimbal, bowl, dish and scoop from Orson & Blake Collectables

bamboo basket from Morris Home & Garden Wares; plate and bowls from Made in Japan

MONGOLIAN LAMB STIR-FRY

1kg lamb fillets, thinly sliced
1 teaspoon five spice powder
2 teaspoons sugar
1 tablespoon cornflour
⅓ cup (80ml) light soy sauce
1 tablespoon black bean sauce
3 cloves garlic, crushed
1 egg, lightly beaten
⅓ cup (80ml) peanut oil
4 medium (600g) onions, sliced
2 cups (160g) bean sprouts
¼ teaspoon sesame oil
1½ teaspoons cornflour, extra
½ cup (125ml) beef stock
4 green shallots, chopped

1. Combine lamb, spice, sugar, cornflour, half the sauces, garlic and egg, mix well. Cover, refrigerate 30 minutes.

2. Heat half the peanut oil in wok or large pan, add onions, stir-fry until just soft, stir in sprouts, remove. Heat remaining peanut oil in wok, stir-fry lamb in batches until browned and tender.

3. Return lamb to wok with remaining sauces, sesame oil and blended extra cornflour and stock, stir until mixture boils and thickens. Stir in shallots and half the onion mixture. Serve lamb on remaining onion mixture.
Serves 4 to 6.

■ Best made just before serving.
■ Freeze: Not suitable.
■ Microwave: Not suitable.

COMBINATION CHOW MEIN

350g thin fresh egg noodles
vegetable oil for deep-frying
1 tablespoon peanut oil
2 (340g) chicken breast
    fillets, sliced
500g uncooked medium prawns,
    shelled, deveined
2 cloves garlic, crushed
2 teaspoons grated fresh ginger
1 medium (150g) onion, sliced
125g Chinese barbecued pork,
    thinly sliced
1 medium (200g) red pepper,
    thinly sliced
125g snow peas, thinly sliced
4 Chinese cabbage leaves,
    shredded
¼ cup (50g) canned drained
    bamboo shoots, sliced
4 green shallots, sliced
1½ cups (120g) bean sprouts
2 tablespoons salt-reduced
    soy sauce
3 teaspoons hoisin sauce
2 teaspoons cornflour
½ cup (125ml) chicken stock

2. Heat half the peanut oil in wok or large pan, add chicken in batches, stir-fry until browned and tender, remove. Chop chicken roughly. Add prawns to wok, stir-fry until tender, remove.

3. Heat remaining peanut oil in wok, add garlic, ginger and onion, stir-fry until onion is just soft. Return chicken and prawns to wok with pork, pepper, snow peas, cabbage, bamboo shoots, shallots and then sprouts, stir-fry until combined. Stir in sauces and blended cornflour and stock, stir over heat until mixture boils and thickens. Serve over noodles.
Serves 4 to 6.

- Best made just before serving.
- Freeze: Not suitable.
- Microwave: Not suitable.

1. Deep-fry noodles in hot vegetable oil until puffed and lightly browned; drain on absorbent paper.

Tray from Morris Home & Garden Wares

SZECHUAN BEEF WITH WATER SPINACH

700g beef rump steak, thinly sliced
2 teaspoons cornflour
1 tablespoon salt-reduced
soy sauce
½ teaspoon sesame oil
1 tablespoon Chinese cooking wine
1 teaspoon finely grated
fresh ginger
1 clove garlic, crushed
1 bunch (about 300g) water spinach
1 tablespoon peanut oil
2 large (400g) onions, sliced
1½ cups (120g) bean sprouts
150g snow peas, halved
1 tablespoon oyster sauce
2 tablespoons chicken stock
1 tablespoon Szechuan pepper

1. Place beef in large bowl, add combined cornflour, soy sauce, sesame oil, wine, ginger and garlic; mix well. Cover, refrigerate 3 hours or overnight.

2. Snap off and discard tough ends of spinach. Snap spinach into bite-sized pieces, rinse under cold water; drain.

3. Heat half the peanut oil in wok or large pan, add beef mixture in batches, stir-fry until beef is browned and tender; remove, cover to keep warm.

4. Heat remaining peanut oil in wok, add onions, stir-fry until onions are just soft. Return beef to wok with sprouts, snow peas, oyster sauce, stock, pepper and spinach, stir until spinach is wilted and beef heated through.
Serves 6.

■ Best made just before serving.
■ Freeze: Not suitable.
■ Microwave: Not suitable.

Bowl from Made in Japan; fabric from St James Furnishings

CITRUS FRIED BEEF

2 pieces dried citrus peel
700g beef rump steak, thinly sliced
2 tablespoons soy bean paste
2 tablespoons dry sherry
1 tablespoon thick soy sauce
1 tablespoon dark soy sauce
1½ bunches (400g) asparagus
2 teaspoons sesame oil
2 cloves garlic, crushed
2 teaspoons finely chopped
   fresh ginger
1 tablespoon peanut oil
4 green shallots, finely chopped
1 tablespoon brown sugar
2 teaspoons hot chilli sauce

3. Snap off and discard coarse ends from asparagus; cut asparagus into 5cm pieces. Heat sesame oil in wok or large pan, add garlic and ginger, stir-fry until fragrant. Add asparagus, stir-fry until just tender; remove.

1. Place peel in small heatproof bowl, cover with boiling water, stand 20 minutes. Drain peel, reserving 2 tablespoons of the liquid, slice peel thinly.

4. Heat peanut oil in wok, add half the beef mixture, stir-fry until almost tender; remove. Repeat with remaining beef mixture.

2. Place beef in large bowl, add combined peel, reserved liquid, paste, sherry and soy sauces, mix well. Cover, refrigerate 30 minutes.

5. Return beef to wok, add asparagus, shallots, sugar and chilli sauce, stir until heated through.
Serves 4 to 6.

■ Best made just before serving.
■ Freeze: Marinated beef suitable.
■ Microwave: Not suitable.

Fabric from St James Furnishings; basket and small wooden container from Accoutrement

SEAFOOD

The subtle flavours of Chinese cooking are especially good when matched with fresh seafood. In these recipes, we show you the secrets of crisp-skinned whole fish, crystal prawns, squid stir-fry, delicious ginger chilli crab, combination seafood rice, and more. They're all so easy to make and are wonderfully tasty.

FISH CUTLETS IN RED SAUCE

2 egg whites, lightly beaten
1/2 teaspoon cracked black peppercorns
1/3 cup (50g) cornflour
4 x 230g blue-eyed cod cutlets
vegetable oil for deep-frying
1 tablespoon peanut oil
1 bunch (600g) choy sum, coarsely chopped
1 clove garlic, thinly sliced
1/4 cup (60ml) salt-reduced soy sauce
1 tablespoon oyster sauce
2 tablespoons rice wine
1 tablespoon sugar
2 teaspoons grated fresh ginger
2 teaspoons cornflour, extra
1/2 cup (125ml) vegetable stock

1. Combine egg whites, pepper and cornflour in bowl, dip cutlets separately in mixture. Deep-fry cutlets in batches in hot vegetable oil until crisp and cooked through, drain on absorbent paper.

2. Heat peanut oil in wok or large pan, add choy sum and garlic, stir-fry until choy sum is just wilted, remove; cover to keep warm.

3. Add sauces, wine, sugar, ginger and blended extra cornflour and stock, stir over heat until mixture boils and thickens. Add cutlets, cook until heated through. Serve with choy sum.
Serves 4.

■ Best made just before serving.
■ Freeze: Not suitable.
■ Microwave: Not suitable.

CRYSTAL PRAWNS WITH CHOY SUM

1kg uncooked large prawns
2 teaspoons salt
2 litres (8 cups) water
1 egg white
3 teaspoons cornflour
1 large (180g) carrot
1 bunch (250g) asparagus
200g thick rice stick noodles
vegetable oil for shallow-frying
1 tablespoon peanut oil
1 tablespoon grated fresh ginger
2 cloves garlic, crushed
1 bunch (600g) choy sum, chopped
1 teaspoon sugar
2 teaspoons plum sauce
2 tablespoons oyster sauce
¼ cup (60ml) dry sherry
½ teaspoon sesame oil
1½ teaspoons cornflour, extra
⅓ cup (80ml) vegetable stock

3. Cut carrot into wedges. Snap off and discard tough ends of asparagus; cut asparagus into 5cm pieces. Boil, steam or microwave carrot and asparagus separately until just tender, rinse under cold water, drain.

4. Place noodles in heatproof bowl, cover with boiling water, stand about 20 minutes or until noodles are soft. Drain noodles, cover to keep warm.

1. Shell prawns; cut prawns down the back, cutting nearly all the way through; remove veins. Combine prawns, salt and water in large bowl, stir 1 minute. Rinse prawns well under cold water, drain on absorbent paper.

5. Heat vegetable oil in wok or large pan, shallow-fry prawns in batches until prawns are just tender, drain on absorbent paper. Heat peanut oil in wok or large pan, add ginger and garlic, stir-fry until fragrant. Add carrot, asparagus and choy sum, stir-fry until choy sum is just wilted. Stir in combined sugar, sauces, sherry, sesame oil and blended extra cornflour and stock, stir until mixture boils and thickens. Stir in prawns and noodles, stir until heated through.
Serves 4.

2. Combine egg white and cornflour in large bowl, add prawns, stir to coat with mixture; cover, refrigerate 1 hour.

- Best made just before serving.
- Freeze: Not suitable.
- Microwave: Carrot and asparagus suitable.

CORIANDER GINGER SQUID STIR-FRY

1.5kg squid hoods
¼ cup chopped fresh
coriander leaves
¼ cup (60ml) Chinese
barbecue sauce
2 tablespoons sweet chilli sauce
¼ cup (60ml) rice vinegar
3 cloves garlic, crushed
1 tablespoon grated fresh ginger
2 tablespoons peanut oil

2. Combine squid with coriander, sauces, vinegar, garlic and ginger in bowl; mix well. Cover, refrigerate 2 hours.

3. Heat oil in wok or large pan, stir-fry squid in batches with some of the marinade for about 1 minute, or until squid is just tender. Return squid to wok, stir-fry until heated through. Serves 6.

■ Best made just before serving.
■ Freeze: Not suitable.
■ Microwave: Not suitable.

1. Cut squid hoods open, score shallow diagonal slashes in criss-cross pattern on inside surface; cut squid into 3cm x 5cm pieces.

PRAWNS AND VEGETABLES WITH NOODLES

450g hokkien noodles
800g uncooked king prawns
1 tablespoon peanut oil
3 cloves garlic, crushed
1 teaspoon finely chopped
   fresh ginger
1 large (350g) red pepper, sliced
200g oyster mushrooms, halved
3 cups (240g) shredded
   Chinese cabbage
1 bunch (360g) Chinese broccoli,
   shredded
1 cup (80g) bean sprouts
1 teaspoon cracked black
   peppercorns
1 tablespoon rice vinegar
2 tablespoons oyster sauce
1 tablespoon light soy sauce
2 tablespoons chopped fresh
   garlic chives

1. Add noodles to large pan of boiling water, boil, uncovered, 2 minutes, drain. Shell and devein prawns, leaving tails intact.

2. Heat oil in wok or large pan, add garlic, ginger, red pepper, mushrooms and prawns, stir-fry until prawns are almost tender.

3. Add noodles, vegetables and combined remaining ingredients, stir-fry until cabbage is just wilted.

Serves 6.
■ Best made just before serving.
■ Freeze: Not suitable.
■ Microwave: Not suitable.

GINGER CHILLI CRAB

2 x 1.5kg uncooked mud crabs
2 teaspoons peanut oil
4 green shallots, chopped
2 tablespoons grated fresh ginger
3 cloves garlic, crushed
3 small fresh red chillies, chopped
2 tablespoons rice vinegar
3/4 cup (180ml) fish stock
1 tablespoon palm sugar
1 tablespoon light soy sauce
1 teaspoon cornflour
2 teaspoons water

3. Heat oil in wok or large pan, add shallots, ginger, garlic and chillies, stir-fry until fragrant.

1. Place live crabs in freezer for at least 2 hours; this is the most humane way of killing a crab. Slide a sharp strong knife under top of shell at back of crabs, lever off shell and discard.

4. Add vinegar, stock, sugar and sauce, bring to boil, stir in blended cornflour and water, stir until mixture boils and thickens. Add crab, cover, cook 15 minutes, stirring occasionally. Serves 2 to 4.

■ Best made just before serving.
■ Freeze: Not suitable.
■ Microwave: Not suitable.

2. Remove and discard gills, wash crabs thoroughly. Chop body into quarters with cleaver. Remove claws and nippers, chop nippers into large pieces.

Stone platter and rope hammock from Orson & Blake Collectables

PRAWNS WITH CHILLI OIL

2 tablespoons peanut oil
8 (200g) spring onions, halved
3 cloves garlic, crushed
2 teaspoons finely chopped
   fresh ginger
vegetable oil for deep-frying
100g thin rice stick noodles
1kg uncooked medium prawns
1 teaspoon chilli oil
2 teaspoons sesame oil
2 tablespoons fresh coriander
   leaves

DRESSING
2 tablespoons rice vinegar
1 tablespoon salt-reduced
   soy sauce
2 teaspoons Chinese cooking wine
1 teaspoon lemon juice
1 teaspoon sugar
1 small fresh red chilli, sliced

Fabric from St James Furnishings

1. Heat half the peanut oil in wok or large pan, add onions, garlic and ginger, stir-fry about 2 minutes or until onions are just soft, remove.

2. Heat vegetable oil in wok, carefully add noodles. Deep-fry noodles until they puff and rise to the surface (this will take about 4 seconds); remove immediately with tongs, drain on absorbent paper.

3. Shell and devein prawns, leaving tails intact. Heat combined chilli oil, sesame oil and remaining peanut oil in wok, add prawns in batches, stir-fry until prawns are just tender, stir in onion mixture. Serve prawns on crisp noodles, drizzle with dressing, sprinkle with coriander leaves.

4. Dressing: Combine all ingredients in jar; shake well.
Serves 4.

■ Best made just before serving.
■ Freeze: Not suitable.
■ Microwave: Not suitable.

CRISPY FISH WITH TOMATOES

4 large (360g) egg tomatoes
1cm piece fresh ginger, peeled
800g ling fillets
¼ cup (35g) cornflour
½ teaspoon salt
vegetable oil for deep-frying
1 tablespoon peanut oil
1 teaspoon sesame oil
2 cloves garlic, crushed
2 tablespoons dry sherry
2 tablespoons tomato sauce
1 tablespoon light soy sauce
2 teaspoons hot chilli sauce
1 teaspoon thick soy sauce

1. Cut tomatoes into thin wedges; remove seeds and cores. Cut ginger into thin strips. Cut fish into 3cm pieces, toss in combined cornflour and salt.

3. Heat peanut and sesame oils in wok or large pan, add garlic and ginger, stir-fry until ginger is crisp. Add tomatoes, sherry and sauces, simmer, uncovered, about 1 minute or until mixture is slightly thickened. Add fish, stir gently to coat with sauce, simmer, uncovered, until fish is heated through.
Serves 4.

■ Best made close to serving.
■ Freeze: Not suitable.
■ Microwave: Not suitable.

2. Deep-fry fish in batches in hot vegetable oil until fish is crisp and cooked through; drain on absorbent paper.

BAKED FISH WITH BLACK BEAN SAUCE

1½ tablespoons packaged salted
   black beans
1 tablespoon peanut oil
¼ teaspoon sesame oil
1 clove garlic, crushed
1 teaspoon finely grated
   fresh ginger
4 green shallots, sliced
⅔ cup (160ml) chicken stock
1 tablespoon hoisin sauce
3 teaspoons thick soy sauce
2 teaspoons brown sugar
800g whole red snapper
2 long sticks celery
1 small (150g) red pepper,
   thinly sliced
⅔ bunch (400g) Chinese mustard
   cabbage, shredded

1. Rinse beans under cold water for 1 minute, drain; lightly mash beans.

2. Heat oils in wok or pan, add beans, garlic and ginger, stir-fry until fragrant.

3. Add shallots then combined stock, sauces and sugar, simmer, uncovered, about 1 minute or until mixture is slightly thickened.

4. Cut 3 deep slits in each side of fish, place fish on top of celery sticks in baking dish so that fish does not touch base of dish. Pour bean mixture over fish, top with pepper.

5. Bake, covered, in moderate oven 25 minutes. Top fish with cabbage, bake, covered, further 5 minutes or until fish is cooked. Serve fish with pepper, cabbage and some of the pan juices. Serves 2 to 4.

- Best made close to serving.
- Freeze: Not suitable.
- Microwave: Not suitable.

Wooden fish from Morris Home & Garden Wares; white platter from Accoutrement

COMBINATION SEAFOOD FRIED RICE

You will need to cook about 1¹/₃ cups (265g) long-grain rice for this recipe.

4 cups cooked long-grain rice
2 teaspoons peanut oil
2 eggs, lightly beaten
500g uncooked medium prawns
250g baby octopus
250g squid hoods
1 tablespoon peanut oil, extra
2 cloves garlic, crushed
3 teaspoons grated fresh ginger
250g scallops, halved
100g Chinese sausage, sliced
½ cup (60g) frozen peas
4 green shallots, sliced
**2 tablespoons salt-reduced
  soy sauce**

1. Spread rice over shallow tray, cover with a cloth, refrigerate overnight.

2. Heat half the oil in wok or large pan, add half the eggs, swirl wok so eggs form a thin omelette over base, cook until set, remove; cool. Repeat with remaining oil and egg mixture. Roll omelettes tightly, slice thinly.

Plate and candleholder from Orson & Blake Collectables; fabric from Alexandra McKenzie Interiors

3. Shell and devein prawns, leaving tails intact. Cut heads from octopus just below eyes, remove beaks. Wash octopus; cut in half.

4. Cut squid hoods open, score shallow diagonal slashes in criss-cross pattern on inside surface; cut into 4cm pieces.

Serves 4 to 6.

- ■ Rice best prepared the night before using.
- ■ Storage: Covered, in refrigerator.
- ■ Freeze: Cooked rice suitable.
- ■ Microwave: Rice suitable.

5. Heat a little of the extra oil in wok, add garlic and ginger, stir-fry 1 minute. Add prawns, stir-fry over high heat until just tender; remove. Repeat cooking in batches with remaining oil, octopus, squid and scallops.

6. Return seafood to wok with rice, sausage, peas, shallots, omelettes and sauce, stir-fry until heated through.

CRISP-SKINNED CHILLI FISH

800g whole bream or snapper
2 cloves garlic, crushed
¼ cup (35g) cornflour
vegetable oil for deep-frying
1 tablespoon peanut oil
4 small fresh red chillies, sliced
2 cloves garlic, crushed, extra
2 teaspoons grated fresh ginger
¼ cup (55g) sugar
1 tablespoon red vinegar
2 tablespoons rice wine
1 tablespoon light soy sauce
¾ cup (180ml) vegetable stock
2 teaspoons cornflour, extra
1 tablespoon water
1 small (70g) carrot, thinly sliced
1 small (150g) red pepper,
    thinly sliced
80g snow peas, thinly sliced

Small bowl from Orson & Blake Collectables

1. Make 5 small shallow diagonal cuts across both sides of fish. Spread fish with garlic, then thickly coat with cornflour. Heat vegetable oil in wok or large pan to smoking point, add fish, deep-fry until fish is crisp and cooked through. Remove fish carefully to absorbent paper, cover to keep warm.

2. Heat peanut oil in wok or large pan, add chillies, extra garlic and ginger, cook, stirring, until fragrant. Add sugar, cook 30 seconds, without stirring. Add vinegar, wine, sauce and stock, then blended extra cornflour and water, stir over heat until sauce boils and thickens.

3. Boil, steam or microwave combined carrot, pepper and snow peas until just tender. Serve fish on vegetables, topped with sauce.
Serves 2 to 4.

■ Best made just before serving.
■ Freeze: Not suitable.
■ Microwave: Vegetables suitable.

SQUIRREL FISH

8 (1kg) bream fillets with skin
¼ cup (35g) cornflour
3 teaspoons coarsely ground
   black peppercorns
vegetable oil for deep-frying

SWEET AND SOUR SAUCE
1 teaspoon peanut oil
2 cloves garlic, crushed
2 teaspoons grated fresh ginger
3 green shallots, sliced
2 tablespoons salt-reduced
   soy sauce
1 tablespoon tomato sauce
2 teaspoons sugar
¼ cup (60ml) chicken stock
2 tablespoons sweet sherry
2 tablespoons rice vinegar
2 teaspoons cornflour
1 tablespoon water

1. Cut shallow diagonal slashes in criss-cross pattern on fleshy side of each fillet.

2. Combine cornflour and pepper in bowl, toss fillets separately in cornflour mixture. Deep-fry fillets in batches in hot oil until lightly browned and cooked through; drain on absorbent paper. Serve with sweet and sour sauce.

3. **Sweet and Sour Sauce:** Heat oil in small pan, add garlic, ginger and shallots, cook, stirring, until fragrant. Add combined sauces, sugar, stock, sherry and vinegar, then blended cornflour and water, stir over heat until mixture boils and thickens.
Serves 6.

■ Fish best cooked just before serving. Sweet and sour sauce can be made a day ahead.
■ Storage: Covered, in refrigerator.
■ Freeze: Not suitable.
■ Microwave: Not suitable.

VEGETARIAN

Lighten up dinner time with these tasty dishes in which the flavours of fresh vegetables are combined with delicious sauces and spices. Vegetables are finely chopped so they cook quickly, while bean curd (tofu) and a range of different noodles are added to many of the recipes to make them well-balanced meals.

VEGETARIAN SANG CHOY BOW

6 Chinese dried mushrooms
2 tablespoons peanut oil
2 cloves garlic, crushed
1 large (180g) carrot, finely chopped
125g fresh baby corn,
    finely chopped
190g packet fried bean curd,
    finely chopped
10 (30g) canned drained water
    chestnuts, chopped
1 tablespoon canned drained
    chopped bamboo shoots
200g oyster mushrooms,
    finely chopped
2 tablespoons chopped fresh
    garlic chives
1 bunch (about 300g) water spinach,
    finely chopped
2 tablespoons hoisin sauce
2 tablespoons light soy sauce
1/3 cup (80ml) water
8 large lettuce leaves

1. Place mushrooms in heatproof bowl, cover with boiling water, stand 20 minutes. Drain mushrooms, discard stems, chop caps.

2. Heat oil in wok or large pan, add garlic, carrot, corn, bean curd, chestnuts, bamboo shoots, mushrooms and chives, stir-fry 2 minutes. Add spinach and combined sauces and water, stir until spinach is wilted. Serve in lettuce leaf cups.
Serves 4.

■ Best made just before serving.
■ Freeze: Not suitable.
■ Microwave: Not suitable.

VEGETABLE AND BEAN THREAD NOODLE STIR-FRY

3 dried cloud ear mushrooms
100g bean thread vermicelli noodles
2 tablespoons peanut oil
3 cloves garlic, crushed
230g can water chestnuts, drained, thickly sliced
1 large (180g) carrot, thinly sliced
1 bunch (430g) choy sum, chopped
125g fresh baby corn, halved
1 tablespoon cornflour
½ cup (125ml) vegetable stock
¼ cup (60ml) hoisin sauce
2 tablespoons light soy sauce
1 teaspoon hot chilli sauce

2. Heat oil in wok or large pan, add garlic, chestnuts and carrot, stir-fry until carrot is almost tender. Add choy sum and corn, stir-fry until corn is almost tender. Add mushrooms and noodles, stir-fry until heated through.

1. Place mushrooms in heatproof bowl, cover with boiling water, stand 20 minutes. Drain mushrooms, reserve ⅓ cup (80ml) of the liquid. Discard stems, slice caps thinly. Place noodles in heatproof bowl, cover with boiling water, stand 5 minutes. Drain noodles well, chop roughly.

3. Blend cornflour with reserved mushroom liquid in jug, stir in stock and sauces. Add sauce mixture to wok, stir over heat until mixture boils and thickens.
Serves 4.

■ Best made just before serving.
■ Freeze: Not suitable.
■ Microwave: Not suitable.

Jars from Blues Point Living

BEAN CURD WITH CHILLI PEANUT SAUCE

vegetable oil for deep-frying
500g packet firm bean
   curd (tofu), chopped
1 tablespoon peanut oil
2 small (300g) red peppers, sliced
160g sugar snap peas
1 bunch (500g) English spinach
2 cups (160g) bean sprouts
2 cloves garlic, crushed
3 small fresh red chillies, sliced
2 teaspoons sambal oelek
1/4 cup (60ml) crunchy peanut butter
2 teaspoons palm sugar
1 tablespoon Chinese cooking wine
1 tablespoon hoisin sauce
1 tablespoon thick sweet soy sauce
1 tablespoon mild sweet chilli sauce
3/4 cup (180ml) water
1/3 cup (50g) unsalted
   roasted peanuts
4 green shallots, chopped
1 tablespoon chopped fresh
   coriander leaves

1. Heat vegetable oil in wok or large pan, add bean curd in batches, deep-fry until browned, drain bean curd on absorbent paper.

2. Heat peanut oil in wok or large pan, add peppers, peas, spinach and sprouts to wok, stir-fry until just tender, remove; cover to keep warm.

3. Add garlic and chillies to wok, stir-fry until fragrant. Add combined sambal oelek, peanut butter, sugar, wine, sauces, water and peanuts, stir over heat until sauce boils. Add shallots, coriander and bean curd, stir until heated through. Serve bean curd and sauce on vegetables.
Serves 4.

■ Best made just before serving.
■ Freeze: Not suitable.
■ Microwave: Not suitable.

Square plate from Kitchen Kapers

HOT 'N' SPICY BEAN CURD ON NOODLES

1kg fresh rice noodles
500g packet firm bean curd (tofu)
2 teaspoons peanut oil
2 cloves garlic, crushed
2 teaspoons finely grated
  fresh ginger
2 sticks celery, thinly sliced
2 medium (240g) carrots,
  thinly sliced
1 medium (200g) red pepper,
  thinly sliced
6 green shallots, sliced
1/2 cup (125ml) vegetable stock
1 tablespoon hot chilli sauce
1 tablespoon Chinese
  barbecue sauce
1/2 teaspoon sugar
1 teaspoon soy bean paste
2 teaspoons Chinese cooking wine
1 teaspoon cornflour
1 tablespoon water

1. Add noodles to pan of boiling water, boil 2 minutes. Drain noodles, cover to keep warm.

2. Cut bean curd into 2cm pieces, place in heatproof bowl, cover with boiling water, stand 2 minutes; drain well.

3. Heat oil in wok or large pan, add garlic and ginger, stir-fry 1 minute. Add celery, carrots and pepper, stir-fry until carrots are just tender. Add shallots, stock, sauces, sugar, paste, wine and blended cornflour and water, stir over heat until mixture boils and thickens. Add bean curd to vegetable mixture, stir gently until heated through. Serve bean curd mixture on noodles.
Serves 4 to 6.

■ Best made just before serving.
■ Freeze: Not suitable.
■ Microwave: Not suitable.

TRIPLE MUSHROOM OMELETTE

12 Chinese dried mushrooms
3 dried cloud ear mushrooms
2 teaspoons peanut oil
6 green shallots, sliced
2 teaspoons grated fresh ginger
2 cloves garlic, crushed
1/2 medium (100g) red
pepper, chopped
100g button mushrooms, sliced
3/4 cup (60g) bean sprouts
1/4 cup (40g) pine nuts, toasted
90g snow peas, thinly sliced
1 tablespoon salt-reduced
soy sauce
1 tablespoon oyster sauce
1 tablespoon water
10 eggs, lightly beaten
1/3 cup (80ml) water, extra

SPICY SAUCE
2 small fresh red chillies,
finely sliced
1/4 cup (60ml) Chinese
barbecue sauce
1/3 cup (80ml) water

1. Place dried mushrooms in small heatproof bowl, cover with boiling water, stand 20 minutes. Drain mushrooms, discard stems, slice caps thinly.

2. Heat oil in wok or large pan, add shallots, ginger, garlic, pepper and all mushrooms, stir-fry until pepper is just soft. Add sprouts, pine nuts, snow peas and combined sauces and water, stir until peas are just tender.

3. Whisk eggs with extra water in medium bowl. Lightly oil 24cm heavy-based omelette pan, heat pan, add 1/3 cup (80ml) of the egg mixture to pan, swirl pan to form a thin omelette over base, cook until set, remove. Repeat with remaining egg mixture. Cover omelettes with foil to keep warm. You need 8 omelettes.

4. Place 1/4 cup of the mushroom mixture on each omelette, fold omelette over filling, then fold over again. Spoon spicy sauce over omelettes to serve.
Spicy Sauce: Combine all ingredients in small pan, stir over heat until mixture boils, simmer, uncovered, about 3 minutes or until slightly thickened. Serves 4.

■ Best made just before serving.
■ Freeze: Not suitable.
■ Microwave: Not suitable.

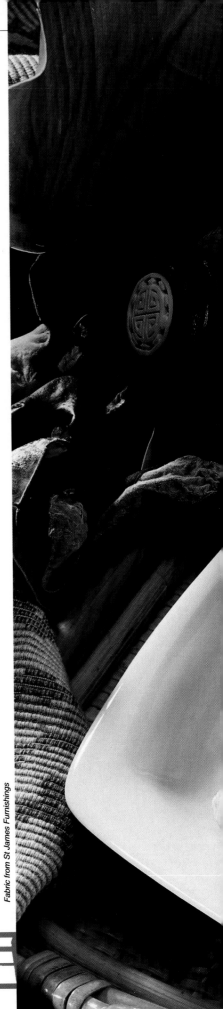

Fabric from St James Furnishings

3. Drain tofu, toss in cornflour, dip in egg. Deep-fry tofu in hot vegetable oil until browned; drain tofu on absorbent paper.

4. Heat peanut oil in wok or large pan, add onion, remaining garlic and remaining ginger, stir-fry until fragrant. Add pepper, carrot and broccoli, stir-fry until vegetables are just tender. Add sauces, sesame oil, curry powder, sprouts and rice, stir until heated through. Serve with tofu.
Serves 4 to 6.

■ Best made just before serving.
■ Freeze: Cooked rice suitable.
■ Microwave: Rice suitable.

Fabric from St James Furnishings

FRIED RICE WITH MARINATED TOFU

You will need to cook 1½ cups (300g) white long-grain rice.

3 cups cooked rice
1½ tablespoons grated fresh ginger
4 cloves garlic, crushed
2 teaspoons hot chilli sauce
2 teaspoons thick sweet soy sauce
297g packet firm tofu (bean curd), coarsely chopped
¼ cup (35g) cornflour
1 egg, lightly beaten
vegetable oil for deep-frying
1½ tablespoons peanut oil
1 medium (150g) onion, sliced
1 small (150g) red pepper, sliced
1 medium (120g) carrot, sliced
100g broccoli florets
1 tablespoon light soy sauce
1 tablespoon hoisin sauce
1 teaspoon sesame oil
2 teaspoons curry powder
2 cups (160g) bean sprouts

1. Spread rice over shallow tray, cover with cloth, refrigerate overnight.

2. Combine half the ginger, half the garlic, chilli sauce and thick sweet soy sauce in bowl, add tofu, stir gently. Cover bowl, refrigerate overnight.

MIXED VEGETABLE CHOW MEIN

5 Chinese dried mushrooms
350g packet thin fresh egg noodles
1 teaspoon sesame oil
¼ cup (60ml) peanut oil
3 cloves garlic, crushed
1 tablespoon grated fresh ginger
1 small fresh red chilli,
    finely chopped
1 medium (120g) carrot, sliced
2 sticks celery, sliced
125g snow peas, sliced
¼ (425g) Chinese cabbage,
    shredded
425g can baby corn, drained, sliced
2 teaspoons cornflour
¼ cup (60ml) water
1 cup (250ml) vegetable stock
2 teaspoons light soy sauce
1 tablespoon hoisin sauce
6 green shallots, sliced

3. Add remaining peanut oil to wok, add garlic, ginger, chilli, mushrooms, carrot and celery, stir-fry until carrot is just tender. Add snow peas, cabbage and corn, stir-fry until cabbage is just wilted.

4. Add blended cornflour and water, stock and sauces, stir over heat until sauce boils and thickens slightly. Add noodles and shallots, stir until heated through.
Serves 4 to 6.

▨ Best made just before serving.
▨ Freeze: Not suitable.
▨ Microwave: Not suitable.

1. Place mushrooms in heatproof bowl, cover with boiling water, stand 20 minutes. Drain mushrooms, discard stems, chop caps finely. Add noodles to large pan of boiling water, drain immediately, rinse under cold water, drain well. Combine noodles with sesame oil in bowl.

2. Add 2 tablespoons of the peanut oil to wok or large pan, add noodles, stir-fry until heated through, remove.

Bowl and cups from Made in Japan

ACCOMPANIMENTS

These tempting dishes will perfectly complement a Chinese banquet or can even become a light meal in themselves. Choose from the many salads, noodle and vegetables dishes or even a Chinese bread. Vegetables should be cooked quickly, so they stay crisp and crunchy and retain all their flavour.

BRAISED VEGETABLES WITH CASHEWS

12 (20g) Chinese dried mushrooms
1 bunch (250g) asparagus
1 tablespoon peanut oil
2 cloves garlic, crushed
1 tablespoon grated fresh ginger
300g broccoli, chopped
2 medium (400g) red peppers, sliced
1/4 (500g) Chinese cabbage, chopped
180g snow peas
230g can water chestnuts, drained, sliced
425g can baby corn spears, drained
2 tablespoons oyster sauce
1/4 cup (60ml) salt-reduced soy sauce
2 teaspoons cornflour
1/3 cup (80ml) water
1 cup (150g) unsalted roasted cashews

1. Place mushrooms in heatproof bowl, cover with boiling water, stand 20 minutes. Drain mushrooms, discard stems, slice caps thinly. Snap off and discard tough ends of asparagus, chop asparagus.

2. Heat oil in wok or large pan, add garlic, ginger, broccoli and peppers, stir-fry until peppers are just soft. Add asparagus, mushrooms, cabbage, snow peas, chestnuts, corn and sauces, stir-fry until vegetables are just tender.

3. Add blended cornflour and water, stir until sauce boils and thickens slightly; stir in nuts.
Serves 6.

■ Best made just before serving.
■ Freeze: Not suitable.
■ Microwave: Not suitable.

Setting from Made in Japan

SINGAPORE-STYLE NOODLES

⅓ cup (40g) dried shrimp
400g rice vermicelli noodles
3 eggs
¼ cup (60ml) peanut oil
1 large (200g) onion, coarsely sliced
2 teaspoons grated fresh ginger
1 small (150g) red pepper, sliced
120g Chinese barbecued
   pork, chopped
½ cup (60g) frozen peas
2 tablespoons curry powder
1 tablespoon light soy sauce
1 teaspoon sesame oil
½ cup (125ml) vegetable stock
2 cups (160g) bean sprouts
4 green shallots, sliced
1 tablespoon chopped fresh
   coriander leaves

1. Place shrimp in heatproof bowl, cover with boiling water, stand 30 minutes, drain. Place noodles in separate heatproof bowl, cover with boiling water, stand 5 minutes, drain.

2. Whisk eggs in small bowl until frothy. Heat 1 tablespoon of the peanut oil in wok or large pan, add egg mixture, stir until just cooked, remove, cover to keep warm.

3. Heat remaining peanut oil in wok, add onion and ginger, cook, stirring, until fragrant. Add pepper and pork, stir-fry 2 minutes. Add shrimp, noodles, peas, curry powder, sauce, sesame oil, stock, sprouts and shallots, stir until heated through. Add egg and coriander, mix gently.
Serves 4 to 6.

■ Best made just before serving.
■ Freeze: Not suitable.
■ Microwave: Not suitable.

Stir-Fried Mushrooms and Water Spinach

8 Chinese dried mushrooms
1 tablespoon peanut oil
2 cloves garlic, crushed
1 teaspoon grated fresh ginger
400g oyster mushrooms, halved
400g button mushrooms, quartered
425g can straw mushrooms,
　drained
2 bunches (900g) Chinese water
　spinach, shredded
5 green shallots, sliced
1 tablespoon light soy sauce
1 tablespoon mild sweet
　chilli sauce
1 tablespoon oyster sauce
1 tablespoon rice vinegar

1. Place dried mushrooms in heat-proof bowl, cover with boiling water, stand 20 minutes. Drain mushrooms, discard stems, slice caps.

2. Heat oil in wok or large pan, add garlic, ginger and all the mushrooms, stir-fry 1 minute. Add spinach, shallots and combined sauces and vinegar, stir-fry until spinach is just wilted. Serves 6.

■ Best made just before serving.
■ Freeze: Not suitable.
■ Microwave: Not suitable.

GREEN ONION BREAD

2 cups (300g) plain flour
1 teaspoon caster sugar
½ teaspoon salt
2 tablespoons vegetable oil
⅔ cup (160ml) water, approximately
¼ cup (60ml) vegetable oil, extra
1 teaspoon sesame oil
6 green shallots, thinly sliced

1. Sift flour, sugar and salt into medium bowl, make well in centre, pour in vegetable oil and enough water to mix to a soft dough.

2. Knead dough lightly on lightly floured surface until just smooth; divide dough into 6 portions. Roll each portion into about a 20cm round, brush with some of the combined extra vegetable oil and sesame oil; sprinkle with shallots, roll up tightly.

3. Shape each roll into a coil, dust with a little flour, flatten slightly with hand; roll out to a 20cm round.

4. Heat 20cm pan, brush with a little more of the combined oils, cook until bread is browned underneath, turn bread, cook other side until crisp. Serve warm or cold.
Makes 6.

■ Best made just before serving.
■ Freeze: Suitable.
■ Microwave: Not suitable.

Stone plate from Orson & Blake Collectables

CHINESE SPINACH SALAD

1 bunch (500g) English spinach
½ bunch (250g) Chinese spinach
1 large (350g) red pepper
1 large (350g) yellow pepper
1 tablespoon peanut oil
1 clove garlic, crushed
400g oyster mushrooms, halved
⅓ cup (50g) canned drained water
    chestnuts, sliced
¼ cup chopped fresh
    coriander leaves

DRESSING
1 tablespoon rice vinegar
1 tablespoon light soy sauce
1 tablespoon mild sweet chilli sauce
1½ tablespoons lemon juice
½ teaspoon sesame oil

1. Wash all spinach, drain, remove stems. Tear English spinach leaves in half. Cut peppers into thin 5cm slices.

2. Heat oil in wok or large pan, add garlic, mushrooms and Chinese spinach, stir-fry until spinach is just wilted.

3. Combine mushroom mixture, English spinach, peppers, chestnuts and coriander in large bowl. Add dressing; mix gently.
Dressing: Combine all ingredients in jar; shake well.

Serves 6.

■ Best made just before serving.
■ Freeze: Not suitable.
■ Microwave: Not suitable.

CHINESE BROCCOLI WITH CRISP FRIED GARLIC

**5 large cloves garlic, peeled
vegetable oil for deep-frying
2 bunches (1kg) Chinese broccoli
½ cup (125ml) oyster sauce
1 tablespoon peanut oil
2 teaspoons sugar**

1. Slice garlic very thinly. Deep-fry garlic in hot vegetable oil in medium pan until golden; drain on absorbent paper.

2. Trim tough ends from broccoli, cut broccoli into 7cm lengths. Add broccoli to large pan of boiling water, boil, uncovered, about 3 minutes or until broccoli turns bright green and is just tender; drain well.

3. Combine broccoli, sauce, peanut oil and sugar in large bowl; mix gently. Serve broccoli topped with fried garlic. Serves 4 to 6.

- Garlic can be cooked a day ahead. Broccoli best cooked just before serving.
- Storage: Garlic in airtight container.
- Freeze: Not suitable.
- Microwave: Broccoli suitable.

Setting from Made in Japan

NOODLES WITH ASPARAGUS

2 bunches (500g) asparagus
450g hokkien noodles
1 teaspoon peanut oil
¼ teaspoon chilli oil
2 cloves garlic, crushed
2 teaspoons finely grated
   fresh ginger
1 small fresh red chilli,
   finely chopped
1 tablespoon salt-reduced
   soy sauce
1 tablespoon Chinese
   barbecue sauce
2 teaspoons Chinese cooking wine
2 teaspoons cornflour
¼ cup (60ml) chicken stock
4 green shallots, sliced
¼ cup (30g) dried shrimp

3. Add noodles, sauces, wine and blended cornflour and stock, stir until mixture boils and thickens. Add shallots and shrimp, stir until heated through. Serves 4 to 6.

■ Best made close to serving.
■ Freeze: Not suitable.
■ Microwave: Not suitable.

1. Snap off and discard tough ends of asparagus, chop asparagus. Cook noodles in pan of boiling water about 2 minutes or until tender, drain.

2. Heat oils in wok or large pan, add garlic, ginger and chilli, stir-fry until fragrant. Add asparagus, stir-fry until asparagus is just tender.

Servers and bowl from The Bay Tree Kitchen Shop; fabric from St James Furnishings

HOT AND SOUR NOODLES

450g hokkien noodles
1 tablespoon peanut oil
3 teaspoons sesame oil
2 tablespoons peanut oil, extra
3 cloves garlic, crushed
½ bunch (50g) garlic
** chives, chopped**
2 teaspoons finely chopped
** fresh ginger**
2 teaspoons crushed dried chillies
⅓ cup (80ml) boiling water
¼ cup (60ml) rice vinegar
1½ tablespoons sugar
2 teaspoons thick soy sauce
2 teaspoons chicken stock powder

1. Add noodles to pan of boiling water, remove from heat, stand about 3 minutes or until noodles are just soft; drain. Return noodles to pan, add peanut and sesame oils; mix well.

2. Heat extra peanut oil in wok or large pan, add garlic, chives, ginger and chillies, stir-fry until fragrant. Add noodles and combined remaining ingredients, stir until heated through.
Serves 4.

■ Best made just before serving.
■ Freeze: Not suitable.
■ Microwave: Not suitable.

RICE NOODLES WITH CHOY SUM

1kg fresh rice noodles
2 teaspoons peanut oil
2 cloves garlic, crushed
1 teaspoon finely grated
 fresh ginger
1 bunch (480g) choy
 sum, chopped
4 green shallots, sliced
½ cup (125ml) hoisin sauce
2 teaspoons cornflour
¼ cup (60ml) chicken stock
2 tablespoons chopped fresh
 coriander leaves

1. Cook noodles in pan of boiling water about 2 minutes or until tender; drain, cover to keep warm.

2. Heat oil in wok or large pan, add garlic and ginger, stir-fry 1 minute. Add choy sum and shallots, stir-fry until choy sum is just wilted.

3. Add sauce and blended cornflour and stock, stir until mixture boils and thickens. Add noodles, stir until heated through. Sprinkle with coriander.
Serves 4 to 6.

■ Best made just before serving.
■ Freeze: Not suitable.
■ Microwave: Not suitable.

NOODLES WITH BABY BOK CHOY AND BLACK BEANS

1 tablespoon packaged salted
  black beans
150g bean thread vermicelli noodles
2 teaspoons peanut oil
2 cloves garlic, crushed
2 teaspoons finely grated
  fresh ginger
1 small fresh red chilli,
  finely chopped
1 bunch (340g) baby bok
  choy, chopped
1 tablespoon Chinese cooking wine
1 tablespoon rice vinegar
2 teaspoons sugar
1 tablespoon salt-reduced
  soy sauce
2 teaspoons cornflour
1 tablespoon water

1. Place beans in bowl, cover with cold water, stand 15 minutes. Drain beans, rinse under cold water several times, drain well; mash beans.

3. Heat oil in wok or large pan, add garlic, ginger, chilli and beans, stir-fry until fragrant. Add bok choy, stir-fry until bok choy is just wilted.

4. Add wine, vinegar, sugar, sauce and blended cornflour and water, stir until mixture boils and thickens. Add noodles, stir until heated through. Serves 4 to 6.

■ Best made just before serving.
■ Freeze: Not suitable.
■ Microwave: Not suitable.

2. Place noodles in heatproof bowl, cover with boiling water, stand 5 minutes, drain; chop roughly.

Bowl from The Bay Tree Kitchen Shop

GREEN VEGETABLES WITH CLOUD EAR MUSHROOMS

1 bunch (250g) asparagus
300g broccoli, chopped
1 tablespoon peanut oil
1 teaspoon sesame oil
1 tablespoon grated fresh ginger
2 cloves garlic, crushed
300g green beans, sliced
1 bunch (350g) bok choy, chopped
100g fresh cloud ear mushrooms,
    finely shredded
3 green shallots, sliced
1/4 cup (60ml) Chinese
    barbecue sauce
1 teaspoon hot chilli sauce
1 tablespoon salt-reduced
    soy sauce
3 teaspoons cornflour
2/3 cup (160ml) water

1. Snap off and discard tough ends of asparagus, slice asparagus. Place broccoli in heatproof bowl, cover with boiling water, stand 2 minutes; drain, rinse under cold water, drain well.

2. Heat oils in wok or large pan, add ginger and garlic, stir-fry until fragrant. Add asparagus, broccoli, beans, bok choy and mushrooms, stir-fry until vegetables are just tender.

3. Add shallots, combined sauces and blended cornflour and water, stir until mixture boils and thickens slightly. Serves 4 to 6.

■ Best made close to serving.
■ Freeze: Not suitable.
■ Microwave: Not suitable.

Black plate from Corso de' Fiori; fabric from South Pacific Fabrics

PICKLED CUCUMBER SALAD

1 small fresh red chilli, chopped
⅓ cup (80ml) white vinegar
¼ cup (55g) sugar
¼ teaspoon chilli oil
4 large (650g) Lebanese cucumbers

1. Combine chilli, vinegar, sugar and oil in pan, stir over heat until sugar is dissolved, cool.

2. Using a vegetable peeler, peel thin strips from cucumbers. Combine cucumbers and vinegar mixture in bowl, mix gently; cover, refrigerate 3 hours or overnight. Just before serving, drain cucumbers, discard liquid. Serves 4.

■ Recipe can be made a day ahead.
■ Storage: Covered, in refrigerator.
■ Freeze: Not suitable.
■ Microwave: Not suitable.

Setting from Orson & Blake Collectables

CABBAGE WITH GINGER AND DRIED SHRIMP

½ cup (60g) dried shrimp
2 tablespoons peanut oil
3 cloves garlic, crushed
2 teaspoons grated fresh ginger
1 medium (1.2kg) Chinese
  cabbage, chopped
1 small (150g) red pepper,
  thinly sliced
2 tablespoons cornflour
2 cups (500ml) chicken stock
¼ cup (60ml) light soy sauce
1 teaspoon sugar
3 green shallots, sliced

1. Place shrimp in heatproof bowl, cover with boiling water, stand 30 minutes, drain.

2. Heat oil in wok or large pan, add garlic and ginger, stir-fry until fragrant. Add cabbage, shrimp and pepper, stir-fry until cabbage is just wilted.

3. Blend cornflour with a little of the stock, add to wok with remaining stock, sauce and sugar, stir over heat until mixture boils and thickens. Stir in shallots.
Serves 4 to 6.

▓ Best made close to serving.
▓ Freeze: Not suitable.
▓ Microwave: Not suitable.

NOODLES WITH SESAME AND PEANUTS

250g rice vermicelli noodles
2 tablespoons peanut oil
3 cloves garlic, crushed
½ cup (75g) chopped
    raw peanuts
¾ cup (180ml) chicken stock
2 tablespoons hoisin sauce
1 tablespoon sesame sauce
2 teaspoons light soy sauce
2 tablespoons smooth peanut butter
3 green shallots, sliced

2. Heat oil in wok or large pan, add garlic and peanuts, stir-fry until peanuts are browned. Add combined stock, sauces and peanut butter, stir until heated through.

3. Add noodles and shallots, stir until heated through.
Serves 4.

■ Best made just before serving.
■ Freeze: Not suitable.
■ Microwave: Not suitable.

1. Place noodles in heatproof bowl, cover with boiling water, stand 5 minutes. Rinse noodles under cold water; drain well.

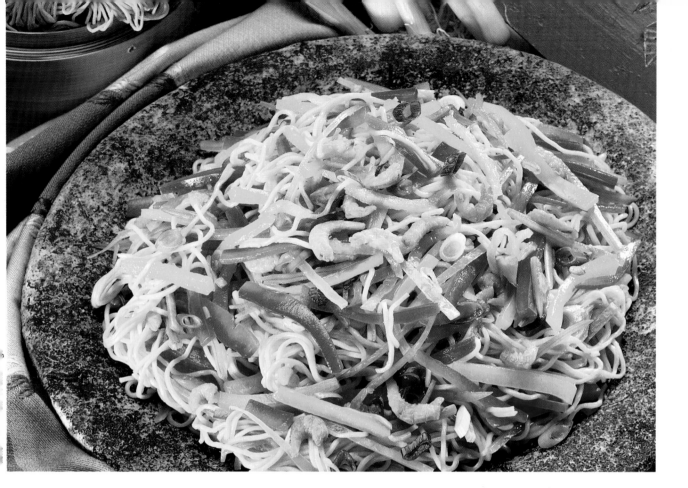

COLD NOODLE SALAD

1/4 cup (30g) dried shrimp
350g thin fresh egg noodles
100g snow peas
2 large (700g) red peppers
1 large (350g) yellow pepper
6 green shallots, sliced
1/2 cup (95g) packaged
    Szechuan pickles

DRESSING
1 tablespoon oyster sauce
1 tablespoon light soy sauce
2 tablespoons rice vinegar
1 1/2 tablespoons lemon juice
1/2 teaspoon chilli oil
1 teaspoon sugar

1. Place shrimp in small heatproof bowl, cover with boiling water, stand 30 minutes, drain.

2. Place noodles in large pan of boiling water, boil 2 minutes, drain, rinse under cold water; drain.

3. Cut peas and peppers into thin 5cm slices. Combine shrimp, noodles, peas, peppers, shallots and pickles in large bowl. Add dressing, mix gently.
Dressing: Combine all ingredients in jar; shake well.
Serves 6.

■ Best made on day of serving.
■ Storage: Covered, in refrigerator.
■ Freeze: Not suitable.
■ Microwave: Not suitable.

SZECHUAN-STYLE SNAKE BEANS WITH PORK

2 bunches (330g) snake beans
2 tablespoons peanut oil
150g minced pork
1 medium (150g) onion,
    thickly sliced
2 cloves garlic, crushed
2 teaspoons grated fresh ginger
1 small fresh red chilli, chopped
1 teaspoon Szechuan pepper,
    toasted, finely crushed
1/3 cup (80ml) oyster sauce
2 teaspoons sugar
2 teaspoons cornflour
3/4 cup (180ml) water
2 teaspoons rice vinegar

3. Add remaining oil to wok, add onion, garlic, ginger, chilli and pepper, stir-fry until fragrant. Add beans, stir-fry until beans are just tender.

1. Trim ends from beans, cut beans into 7cm lengths.

4. Add combined sauce and sugar, then blended cornflour and water, stir until mixture boils and thickens slightly. Add vinegar and pork, stir until pork is heated through.
Serves 4.

- Best made close to serving.
- Freeze: Not suitable.
- Microwave: Not suitable.

2. Heat half the oil in wok or large pan, add pork, stir-fry until well browned, remove from wok.

Fabric from South Pacific Fabrics

SPICY FRIED RICE

You will need to cook about 1 cup (200g) white long-grain rice for this recipe.

3 cups cooked white long-grain rice
2 tablespoons peanut oil
4 eggs, lightly beaten
1 teaspoon sesame oil
1 medium (150g) onion, chopped
2 cloves garlic, crushed
1 tablespoon grated fresh ginger
3 small fresh red chillies, sliced
1 tablespoon sambal oelek
200g cooked shelled small prawns
3/4 cup (90g) frozen peas
3/4 cup (90g) frozen corn
160g Chinese barbecued
**   pork, chopped**
1 tablespoon light soy sauce
1 tablespoon oyster sauce
1 teaspoon five spice powder
1½ cups (120g) bean sprouts

3. Heat remaining peanut oil in wok, add sesame oil, onion, garlic, ginger, chillies and sambal oelek, stir-fry until onion is just soft. Add prawns, peas, corn and pork, stir-fry 1 minute.

4. Add rice, sauces, spice and sprouts, stir until heated through. Add omelettes, mix gently.
Serves 6.

- Best cooked just before serving.
- Freeze: Cooked rice suitable.
- Microwave: Rice suitable.

1. Spread rice over shallow tray, cover with a cloth, refrigerate overnight.

2. Heat 1 teaspoon of the peanut oil in wok or small pan, add half the eggs, swirl wok so eggs form a thin omelette over base, cook until set, remove, cool. Roll omelette, cut into thin strips. Repeat with 1 teaspoon of the remaining peanut oil and remaining eggs.

Wok from Opus Design; fabric from St James Furnishings

KITCHEN NOTES

STIR-FRY BASICS

Once you have a wok, the rest is easy! The large, round, open shape sits easily over the high heat needed for stir-frying, and you can lift, toss and move food around with no problems. Here is a round-up of our most helpful tips and information.

WHICH WOK TO BUY?

Woks come in a variety of shapes, sizes and finishes, ranging from the traditional carbon steel wok to cast iron, stainless steel, non-stick and electric ones. The traditional, round-based woks are great for gas burners, while the flat-based woks are best used on electric stoves. Many woks are available from Asian food stores, while others can be found in most department stores.

SEASONING A WOK

Stainless steel and non-stick woks don't need seasoning. However, carbon steel and cast iron woks need to be seasoned before use.

First, wash the wok in hot, soapy water to remove all traces of grease, then dry wok thoroughly. Heat the wok, add about 2 tablespoons of cooking oil, rub over entire inside surface of wok with absorbent paper. Continue heating the wok for about 10 to 15 minutes, wiping with more paper; cool. Repeat process twice. The wok is now ready to use.

After each use, wash the wok in hot, soapy water; do not scrub with steel wool or harsh abrasives. Dry wok thoroughly by standing it over low heat for a few minutes, then rub or spray a thin layer of cooking oil over the entire surface of wok before storing to avoid rust.

With constant use, the inside surface will darken and become well seasoned. The older, more seasoned the wok becomes, the better it cooks.

WOK CHAN

A wok spatula or chan is a metal, shovel-like utensil used for lifting, tossing and stirring food. Wooden spatulas are best used in non-stick woks as they don't scratch the surface.

WOK BURNERS

Wok burners, portable gas burners and wok-holes for barbecues are all available.

RICE AND NOODLES

Both rice and noodles are indispensable in Chinese cooking. On page 123 we show the noodles we used in this book. Many are interchangeable, so if you can't get the noodles we specify, you can substitute similar noodles; this won't alter the flavour of the dish.

We have not always specified when to serve rice with our recipes, but it is a perfect accompaniment. It can be cooked several ways.

COOKING AND REHEATING RICE

ABSORPTION (STEAMED) METHOD

Combine water and rice in medium heavy-based pan, cover tightly, bring to boil, reduce heat to as low as possible, cook for recommended time. Do not remove lid during cooking. Remove pan from heat, stand, covered, 10 minutes. Fluff rice with a fork.

MICROWAVE METHOD

Combine rice and boiling water in large microwave-safe bowl or jug. Cook, uncovered, on HIGH for recommended time or until rice is tender. Stir halfway through cooking. Cover, stand 5 minutes. Fluff rice with a fork.

BAKED METHOD

Combine rice and boiling water in oven-proof dish, stir well. Cover tightly with foil or lid. Bake in moderate oven for recommended time or until rice is tender. Fluff rice with a fork.

BOILED METHOD

Bring water to boil in large pan, add rice, stir to separate grains, boil, uncovered, for recommended time or until rice is tender; drain.

An electric rice cooker or a rice steamer will also give good, consistent results. Do not rinse cooked rice unless specified in recipes.

REHEATING COOKED RICE

Reheating times will depend on the temperature and quantity of the rice.

● Place rice in colander, stand over pan of simmering water; cover, heat.

● Add just enough water to a frying pan to barely cover base. Bring to the boil, add rice, cover, heat until water is absorbed.

● Spread rice into greased, shallow ovenproof dish, sprinkle with a little water or milk, dot with butter. Cover, heat in moderate oven.

● Heat a little butter or oil in a wok or frying pan, add rice, stir gently with a fork until hot.

● Place rice in a microwave-safe dish, cover, heat on HIGH.

STIR-FRYING TIPS

● Prepare all ingredients before you start to cook.

● For best results, cut meat across the grain as thinly as possible. To do this, wrap meat tightly in plastic wrap, then partly freeze before cutting into wafer-thin slices.

● Heat the wok before adding oil.

● Heat the oil before adding food.

● Stir-fry meat, poultry and seafood over high heat in batches so the food will brown and seal quickly.

● It is important to keep lifting, stirring and moving ingredients in the wok while stir-frying. A wok chan or a wooden spatula is ideal.

● You should also shake the wok while stir-frying. To do this, hold the handle in 1 hand (wear an oven glove for protection against the heat), and you will soon coordinate the shaking and stir-frying actions.

● Stir-fry just before serving.

MARINADES

● If marinating uncooked meat, poultry and seafood, always be sure that any reserved marinade used for a sauce or dressing is brought to the boil before serving.

● Always cover and refrigerate mixtures while they are marinating.

RICE ADVICE

● 1 cup of uncooked white rice = 200g.

● White rice almost triples in bulk during cooking.

● There is no need to wash Australian-grown rice in order to clean it.

● Store uncooked rice, tightly covered, in a cool, dark place. Check the "use by" date for a guide to keeping times.

● Left-over cooked rice can be stored, covered, in the refrigerator for up to 2 days.

● Cooked rice freezes well. Place cooked rice in a freezer bag, press to remove air or use a freezer pump; freeze for up to 2 months.

● Quick-cook rice and ready cooked frozen rice are convenient products when you are in a hurry; look for them in your supermarket.

COOKING TIMES FOR RICE Note: we used an 830 watt microwave oven.

WHITE RICE (LONG- AND SHORT-GRAIN)

METHOD	QUANTITY OF RICE	QUANTITY OF WATER	COOKING TIME
ABSORPTION	1½ cups (300g)	3 cups (750ml)	10 minutes
MICROWAVE	1½ cups (300g)	3 cups (750ml)	10 minutes
BAKED	1½ cups (300g)	2½ cups (625ml)	25 minutes
BOILED	1½ cups (300g)	8 cups (2 litres)	12 minutes

Green shallots

Fresh ginger

GLOSSARY

Here are some terms, names and alternatives to help everyone use and understand our recipes perfectly.

BAKING POWDER: a raising agent consisting of a starch, but mostly cream of tartar and bicarbonate of soda in the proportions of 1 level teaspoon of cream of tartar to ½ level teaspoon bicarbonate of soda. This is equivalent to 2 teaspoons baking powder.

BAMBOO SHOOTS: the tender shoots of bamboo plants; available in cans.

BEAN CURD: see Tofu. Packaged fried bean curd consists of cubes of soft bean curd deep-fried until the surface is brown and crusty and the inside almost dry.

BEANS:

Black beans, salted packaged: fermented, salted soya beans; canned and dried black beans can be used instead. Drain and rinse packaged or canned beans; soak and rinse dried beans. Mash beans when cooking to release flavour.

Green: sometimes called French beans.

Snake: long, thin beans at least 40cm in length. Colour, taste and texture are similar to green beans.

Soya beans in sauce, salted: whole soya beans in a sauce of wheat flour, salt and sugar.

BEAN SPROUTS (bean shoots): we used mung bean sprouts.

BEEF:

Eye-fillet: tenderloin.

Minced: ground beef.

Rump steak: boneless tender cut.

BREADCRUMBS:

Stale: use 1- or 2-day-old bread made into crumbs by grating, blending or processing.

CHILLIES: available in many different types and sizes. Use rubber gloves when chopping fresh chillies as they can burn your skin. Remove seeds and membranes unless you like the heat.

Dried crushed: available from supermarkets and Asian food stores.

Powder: the Asian variety is the hottest and is made from ground chillies; it can be used as a substitute for fresh chillies in the proportion of ½ teaspoon chilli powder to 1 medium chopped fresh chilli.

CHINESE GREEN VEGETABLES: The same vegetable can be called by more than one name, often causing a lot of confusion. We have listed many of the alternative names.

Baby bok choy: more tender than bok choy.

Bok choy (bak choy, pak choi, Chinese white cabbage, Chinese chard): mild, fresh mustard taste; use stems and leaves.

Chinese broccoli (gai lum, Chinese kale): similar to choy sum, but with white flowers; very crunchy.

Chinese cabbage (Peking cabbage, wong nga baak, wong bok): milder taste than Western cabbage.

Chinese spinach (amaranth, yin choy): sold with roots, which are pinkish red; young shoots and leaves are the most tender.

Choy sum (flowering bok choy, flowering white cabbage, bok choy sum): has a mild, mustard-like flavour.

Mustard cabbage (gai choy): has a pungent flavour.

Tat-soi (rosette pak choy, tai gu choy, Chinese flat cabbage): a variety of bok choy, developed to grow close to the ground so it is easily protected from frost.

Water spinach (swamp spinach, long green, ung choy, kang kong): has hollow stems and green, pointed leaves; use leaves and top half of stem.

CHINESE SAUSAGES: highly spiced, bright red, thin pork sausages. The meat is preserved by the high spice content and can be kept at room temperature.

CHIVES: related to the onion and leek, with subtle onion flavour. Chives and flowering chives are interchangeable.

Garlic: have flat leaves and stronger flavour than chives.

CITRUS PEEL: dried tangerine peel, available in Asian food stores.

CORIANDER (cilantro and Chinese parsley): a pungent herb available fresh, ground and in seed form (the seeds are an important ingredient in curry powder). Roots and stems are edible.

CORNFLOUR: cornstarch.

CURRY POWDER: a convenient combination of powdered spices. Consists of chilli, coriander, cumin, fennel, fenugreek and turmeric in varying proportions.

DRIED SHRIMP: dried salted baby prawns.

DUCK:

Breast fillet: has skin but no bone.

Chinese barbecued: available from many Asian food and specialty stores; ready to eat when bought.

ENGLISH SPINACH: a soft-leaved vegetable; young silverbeet can be substituted.

FIVE SPICE POWDER: a pungent mixture of ground spices which includes cinnamon, cloves, fennel, star anise and Szechuan peppers.

FLOUR:

Plain: all-purpose flour.

FRIED BEAN CURD: see Bean Curd.

FRIED GARLIC: we used a thinly sliced, bottled product.

GARLIC: a bulb contains many cloves. Cloves can be crushed, sliced, chopped or used whole.

GINGER:

Fresh, green or root ginger: scrape away skin and grate, chop or slice.

There are 2 ways to keep unused ginger: Peel ginger, cover with dry sherry in jar and refrigerate, or, peel ginger and freeze in airtight container.

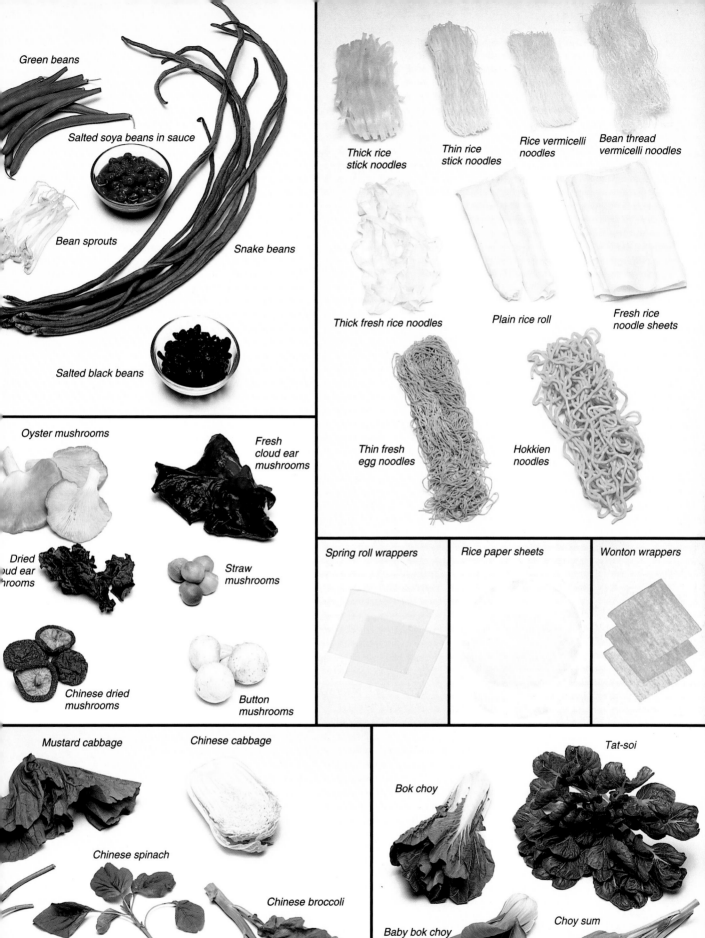

Green beans

Salted soya beans in sauce

Bean sprouts

Snake beans

Salted black beans

Thick rice stick noodles

Thin rice stick noodles

Rice vermicelli noodles

Bean thread vermicelli noodles

Thick fresh rice noodles

Plain rice roll

Fresh rice noodle sheets

Thin fresh egg noodles

Hokkien noodles

Oyster mushrooms

Fresh cloud ear mushrooms

Dried cloud ear mushrooms

Straw mushrooms

Chinese dried mushrooms

Button mushrooms

Spring roll wrappers

Rice paper sheets

Wonton wrappers

Mustard cabbage

Chinese cabbage

Tat-soi

Bok choy

Chinese spinach

Chinese broccoli

Baby bok choy

Choy sum

Water spinach

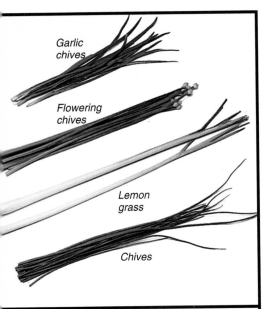

Garlic chives

Flowering chives

Lemon grass

Chives

Coriander seeds

Coriander

Snow pea sprouts

Snow peas

GREEN SHALLOTS: also known as scallions, eschalots and green onions. Do not confuse with the small brown French shallots.

LAMB FILLETS: tenderloin; the smaller piece of meat from a row of loin chops or cutlets.

LEBANESE CUCUMBER: thin-skinned variety also known as the European or burpless cucumber.

LEEK: a member of the onion family, resembles the green shallot but is much larger.

LEMON GRASS: available from Asian food stores and some greengrocers.

LEMON PEPPER SEASONING: a blend of crushed black pepper, lemon, herbs and spices.

LING: a member of the cod family with white, firm, moist flesh; fillets are nearly boneless.

MUD CRAB: mangrove crab.

MUSHROOMS:

Button: small, unopened mushrooms with a delicate flavour.

Cloud ear (wood ear or dried black fungus): swells to about 5 times its dried size when soaked.

Dried Chinese: unique in flavour.

Oyster (abalone): grey-white mushroom shaped like a fan.

Straw: cultivated Chinese mushroom with earthy flavour; sold canned in brine.

NOODLES:

Fresh egg: made from wheat flour and eggs; strands vary in thickness.

Fresh rice: made from rice, vegetable oil and water, and are available as noodle strands, noodle sheets or a plain rice roll. Sheets and roll are interchangeable.

Hokkien: parboiled Asian wheat noodles; they are interchangeable with packaged, freshly steamed Asian-style noodles labelled "Stir-Fry Noodles" in supermarkets.

Rice stick: we used 2 types: a flat, thick variety and a thin variety, both made from rice flour and water.

Vermicelli: we used 2 types: rice vermicelli and bean thread vermicelli made from green beans, broad beans and peas ("cellophane" noodles).

OIL:

Chilli: made by steeping dried chillies in vegetable oil; is intensely hot in flavour.

Peanut: made from ground peanuts, is the most common oil in Asian cooking, but a lighter salad-type of oil can be used.

Sesame: made from roasted, crushed white sesame seeds, used for flavouring.

Vegetable: we used a polyunsaturated vegetable oil.

PEPPERS: capsicum or bell peppers; remove seeds and membranes.

PORK:

American-style spare ribs: well-trimmed mid-loin ribs.

Chinese barbecued: roasted pork fillets available from many Asian food and specialty stores.

Minced: ground.

Spare ribs: cut from the pork belly.

PRAWNS: shrimp.

RICE:

Jasmine: fragrant long-grain rice.

White long-grain: elongated grains.

RICE PAPER SHEETS: available from gourmet shops and shops which specialise in Asian ingredients.

RIND: zest.

SAMBAL OELEK (also ulek or olek): a salty paste made from ground chillies.

SAUCES:

Black bean: made from fermented soya beans, water and wheat flour.

Chinese barbecue: consists of sugar, soya beans, salt, flour starch, vinegar, tomato, garlic, pepper and spice.

Hoisin: a thick, sweet, Chinese barbecue sauce made from salted black beans, onions and garlic.

Hot chilli: we used a hot Chinese variety. It consists of chillies, salt and vinegar; use sparingly.

Mild sweet chilli: made from red chillies, sugar, garlic, salt and vinegar.

Oyster: a rich brown sauce made from oysters cooked in salt and soy sauce, then thickened with starches.

Plum: a dipping sauce made from plums, sugar, chillies and spices.

Satay: we used a satay sauce with a strong peanut aroma and taste; several varieties are available.

Saté: a thin, clear, golden sauce with a pleasant chilli taste and a trace of peanut flavour. It is available only in Asian food stores.

Sesame: consists of crushed sesame seeds, peanuts, starch and vegetable oil.

Soy (or soya): is made from fermented soya beans, wheat flour, salt and water; sugar can be added to make a sweeter variety. Some available in supermarkets; all should be in most Asian food stores.

Tomato: tomato ketchup.

SCALLOPS: we used scallops with cora (roe) attached.

SESAME SEEDS: varieties include whit and black. To toast white sesame seeds spread seeds evenly onto oven tray, toast in moderate oven about 5 minutes or stir in heavy-based pan over heat unt golden brown.

QUICK CONVERSION GUIDE

Wherever you live in the world you can use our recipes with the help of our easy-to-follow conversions for all your cooking needs. These conversions are approximate only. The difference between the exact and approximate conversions of liquid and dry measures amounts to only a teaspoon or two, and will not make any difference to your cooking results.

MEASURING EQUIPMENT

The difference between measuring cups internationally is minimal within 2 or 3 teaspoons' difference. (For the record, 1 Australian metric measuring cup will hold approximately 250ml.) The most accurate way of measuring dry ingredients is to weigh them. When measuring liquids use a clear glass or plastic jug with metric markings.

If you would like the measuring cups and spoons as used in our Test Kitchen, turn to page 128 for details and order coupon. In this book we use metric measuring cups and spoons approved by Standards Australia.

● a graduated set of four cups for measuring dry ingredients; the sizes are marked on the cups.
● a graduated set of four spoons for measuring dry and liquid ingredients; the amounts are marked on the spoons.
● 1 TEASPOON: 5ml.
● 1 TABLESPOON: 20ml.

NOTE: NZ, CANADA, USA AND UK ALL USE 15ml TABLESPOONS.
ALL CUP AND SPOON MEASUREMENTS ARE LEVEL.

DRY MEASURES

METRIC	IMPERIAL
15g	½oz
30g	1oz
60g	2oz
90g	3oz
125g	4oz (¼lb)
155g	5oz
185g	6oz
220g	7oz
250g	8oz (½lb)
280g	9oz
315g	10oz
345g	11oz
375g	12oz (¾lb)
410g	13oz
440g	14oz
470g	15oz
500g	16oz (1lb)
750g	24oz (1½lb)
1kg	32oz (2lb)

LIQUID MEASURES

METRIC	IMPERIAL
30ml	1 fluid oz
60ml	2 fluid oz
100ml	3 fluid oz
125ml	4 fluid oz
150ml	5 fluid oz (¼ pint/1 gill)
190ml	6 fluid oz
250ml	8 fluid oz
300ml	10 fluid oz (½ pint)
500ml	16 fluid oz
600ml	20 fluid oz (1 pint)
1000ml (1 litre)	1¾ pints

WE USE LARGE EGGS WITH AN AVERAGE WEIGHT OF 60g

HELPFUL MEASURES

METRIC	IMPERIAL
3mm	⅛in
6mm	¼in
1cm	½in
2cm	¾in
2.5cm	1in
5cm	2in
6cm	2½in
8cm	3in
10cm	4in
13cm	5in
15cm	6in
18cm	7in
20cm	8in
23cm	9in
25cm	10in
28cm	11in
30cm	12in (1ft)

HOW TO MEASURE

When using the graduated metric measuring cups, it is important to shake the dry ingredients loosely into the required cup. Do not tap the cup on the bench, or pack the ingredients into the cup unless otherwise directed. Level top of cup with knife. When using graduated metric measuring spoons, level top of spoon with knife. When measuring liquids in the jug, place jug on flat surface, check for accuracy at eye level.

OVEN TEMPERATURES

These oven temperatures are only a guide; we've given you the lower degree of heat. Always check the manufacturer's manual.

	C° (Celsius)	F° (Fahrenheit)	Gas Mark
Very slow	120	250	1
Slow	150	300	2
Moderately slow	160	325	3
Moderate	180 – 190	350 – 375	4
Moderately hot	200 – 210	400 – 425	5
Hot	220 – 230	450 – 475	6
Very hot	240 – 250	500 – 525	7

TWO GREAT OFFERS FROM THE AWW HOME LIBRARY

Here's the perfect way to keep your Home Library books in order, clean and within easy reach. More than a dozen books fit into this smart silver grey vinyl folder. PRICE: Australia $11.95; elsewhere $21.95; prices include postage and handling. To order your holder, see the details below.

All recipes in the AWW Home Library are created using Australia's unique system of metric cups and spoons. While it is relatively easy for overseas readers to make any minor conversions required, it is easier still to own this durable set of Australian cups and spoons (photographed). PRICE : Australia: $5.95; New Zealand: $A8.00; elsewhere: $A9.95; prices include postage & handling.
This offer is available in all countries.

TO ORDER YOUR METRIC MEASURING SET OR BOOK HOLDER:

PHONE: Have your credit card details ready. Sydney: (02) 260 0035; **elsewhere in Australia:** 008 252 515 (free call, Mon-Fri, 9am-5pm) or FAX your order to (02) 267 4363 or MAIL your order by photocopying or cutting out and completing the coupon below.

PAYMENT: **Australian residents:** We accept the credit cards listed, money orders and cheques. **Overseas residents:** We accept the credit cards listed, drafts in $A drawn on an Australian bank, also English, New Zealand and U.S. cheques in the currency of the country of issue.
Credit card charges are at the exchange rate current at the time of payment.

Please photocopy and complete coupon and fax or send to:
AWW Home Library Reader Offer, ACP Direct, PO Box 7036, Sydney 2001.

❏ Metric Measuring Set   ❏ Holder

Please indicate number(s) required.

Mr/Mrs/Ms _____

Address _____

_____

Postcode _____ Country_____

Ph: (   ) _____Bus. Hour: _____

I enclose my cheque/money order for $_____ payable to ACP Direct

OR: please charge my:

❏ Bankcard ❏ Visa ❏ MasterCard ❏ Diners Club ❏ Amex

☐☐☐☐☐☐☐☐☐☐☐☐☐☐☐☐ Exp. Date ___/___

Cardholder's signature _____

(Please allow up to 30 days for delivery within Australia. Allow up to 6 weeks for overseas deliveries.)

Both offers expire 31/12/96.   AWSF96

SNOW PEAS: also known as mange tout ('eat all).

SNOW PEA SPROUTS: sprouted seeds of the snow pea.

SOY BEAN PASTE: crushed soya beans with sesame oil and flavourings.

SPRING ONIONS: vegetables with small white bulbs and long green leaves.

SPRING ROLL WRAPPERS: thin white sheets of pastry, sold frozen; thaw before using in a recipe.

SQUID HOODS (or tubes): convenient cleaned squid (calamari).

STAR ANISE: the dried star-shaped fruit of an evergreen tree; it has an aniseed flavour.

STOCK: 1 cup (250ml) stock is the equivalent of 1 cup (250ml) water plus 1 crumbled stock cube (or 1 teaspoon stock powder). If you prefer to make your own fresh stock, see recipes on this page.

SUGAR: we used coarse granulated table sugar, also known as crystal sugar, unless otherwise specified.

Brown: a soft, fine granulated sugar containing molasses.

Caster: also known as superfine; is fine granulated table sugar.

Palm: also known as gula jawa, gula melaka and jaggery; is a brown, crumbly sugar from the coconut palm and has a treacle-like flavour. Substitute brown or black sugar.

SZECHUAN PEPPER (Chinese pepper): red-brown aromatic seeds with a peppery-lemon flavour.

SZECHUAN PICKLES: packaged product consisting of sliced mustard stem, salt and red pepper.

SZECHUAN SEASONING: powdered mix of garlic, salt, ginger, paprika, onion, pepper, chives, red pepper and spices.

TOFU: also known as bean curd or soybean curd, tofu is made from boiled, crushed soya beans in a process similar to cheese-making. Firm tofu is the same as "hard" or "firm" bean curd. Buy tofu as fresh as possible; keep any leftover in the refrigerator under water, which must be changed daily.

TOMATO:

Egg: also known as Roma, Italian or plum tomatoes.

Paste: a concentrated tomato puree used in flavouring soups, stews, sauces and casseroles, etc.

Puree: canned, pureed tomatoes (not tomato paste). Use fresh, peeled, pureed tomatoes as a substitute, if preferred.

VINEGAR:

Brown malt: made from fermented malt and beech shavings.

Red: ingredients include water, rice, glutinous rice and food colour.

Red wine: is based on red wine.

Rice: made from fermented rice. Ingredients list "water and salt" on the variety we used. Several varieties are available.

White: made from spirits of cane sugar.

WATER CHESTNUTS: small, white, crisp bulbs with a brown skin. Canned water chestnuts are peeled and will keep for about a month in the refrigerator.

WINE:

Chinese cooking: the variety we used contains 16% alcohol and 1.5% salt.

Rice: distilled spirits of rice; contains 17.5% alcohol and 1.5% salt; we used "cooking michiu"; dry sherry can be substituted.

WONTON WRAPPERS: gow gee, egg or spring roll wrappers can be substituted.

YEAST: allow 2 teaspoons (7g) dried yeast to each 15g compressed yeast if substituting one for the other.

English spinach

Lebanese cucumber

MAKE YOUR OWN STOCK

If you prefer to make your own stock, these recipes can be made up to 4 days ahead and stored, covered, in the refrigerator. Be sure to remove any fat from the surface after the cooled stock has been refrigerated overnight. If the stock is to be kept longer, it is best to freeze it in smaller quantities. Stock is also available in cans or tetra packs. Stock cubes or powder can be used. As a guide, 1 teaspoon of stock powder or 1 small crumbled stock cube mixed with 1 cup (250ml) water will give a fairly strong stock. Be aware of the salt and fat content of cubes and powders and prepared stocks.

BEEF STOCK
2kg meaty beef bones
2 medium (300g) onions
2 sticks celery, chopped
2 medium (250g) carrots, chopped
3 bay leaves
2 teaspoons black peppercorns
5 litres (20 cups) water
3 litres (12 cups) water, extra
Place bones and unpeeled, chopped onions in baking dish. Bake in hot oven about 1 hour or until bones and onions are well browned. Transfer bones and onions to large pan, add celery, carrots, bay leaves, peppercorns and water, simmer, uncovered, 3 hours. Add extra water, simmer, uncovered, further 1 hour; strain.
Makes about 2.5 litres (10 cups).

FISH STOCK
1.5kg fish bones
3 litres (12 cups) water
1 medium (150g) onion, chopped
2 sticks celery, chopped
2 bay leaves
1 teaspoon black peppercorns
Combine all ingredients in large pan, simmer, uncovered, 20 minutes; strain.
Makes about 2.5 litres (10 cups).

CHINESE CHICKEN STOCK
2kg chicken necks
5 litres (20 cups) water
2 medium (300g) onions, chopped
4 sticks celery, chopped
6cm piece (40g) fresh ginger,
  peeled, sliced
2 teaspoons black peppercorns
Discard skin from chicken necks. Combine all ingredients in large pan, bring to boil. Skim stock then simmer, uncovered, 2 hours. Strain stock through fine sieve into large bowl, discard necks and vegetables. Cool stock, cover, refrigerate overnight. Next day, skim fat from stock.
Makes about 3 litres (12 cups).

VEGETABLE STOCK
2 large (360g) carrots, chopped
2 large (360g) parsnips, chopped
4 medium (600g) onions, chopped
12 sticks celery, chopped
4 bay leaves
2 teaspoons black peppercorns
6 litres (24 cups) water
Combine all ingredients in large pan, simmer, uncovered, 1½ hours; strain.
Makes about 2.5 litres (10 cups).

INDEX